HOW TO SYNDICATE YOUR OWN NEWSPAPER COLUMN

To Ells from

Bob

HOW TO SYNDICATE YOUR OWN NEWSPAPER COLUMN

W. P.
WILLIAMS

AND

JOSEPH H.
VAN ZANDT

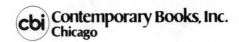

Contemporary Books, Inc.
Chicago

Library of Congress Cataloging in Publication Data

Williams, W. P.   1953-
    How to syndicate your own newspaper column.

    Includes index.
    1. Newspapers—Sections, columns, etc.   2. Journal-
ism—Authorship.   3. Syndicates (Journalism)   I. Van
Zandt, Joseph, 1940-   joint author.   II. Title.
PN4784.C65W5   658.8′09′070442   78-26142
ISBN 0-8092-7380-2
ISBN 0-8092-7379-9 pbk.

Published by Contemporary Books, Inc.
180 North Michigan Avenue, Chicago, Illinois 60601
Manufactured in the United States of America
Library of Congress Catalog Card Number: 78-26142
International Standard Book Number: 0-8092-7380-2 (cloth)
                                    0-8092-7379-9 (paper)

Published simultaneously in Canada by
Beaverbooks
953 Dillingham Road
Pickering, Ontario L1W 1Z7
Canada

Contents

Introduction   *vii*

Part 1: Developing the column   1

1 Why syndicate?   *3*

2 Subject matter   *7*

3 Developing your column idea   *23*

4 Writing the column   *31*

5 A special breed   *41*

6 Putting it all together   *47*

7 Freebies and other "fringe benefits"   *51*

8 Avoiding legal hassles   *61*

Part 2: Selling the column   65

9 The nature of the beast   *67*

10 Selling your ideas   *73*

11 Going it alone   *79*

Conclusion: What to expect   *91*

Index   *93*

Introduction

Most newspapermen have two dreams: The first is to quit their job as reporter, rewrite man, or copy editor some day and head for a cabin in the hills or a deserted beach where they can write the "Great American Novel"; the second dream is to one day become a syndicated columnist. (Make that SYNDICATED columnist.)

Occasionally, we in the newspaper game hear of a former colleague who did take the plunge, quitting his job and going off to write that novel. Usually in the six months or so (depending on how the nest egg holds out) the errant newsman returns, half-finished manuscript and rejection letters in hand, ready to grovel if that's what it will take to get his old job back.

There are exceptions. Once every generation or so the newspaper racket produces a giant the likes of Samuel Clemens or Ernest Hemingway. But let's face it: The odds are about a million to one against you, and a billion to one if you are strictly an amateur.

But that only rules out one of the dreams of newsmen and others who produce journalistic writing (as opposed to purely fiction). While it might seem that becoming a syndicated columnist is even more unlikely, the fact is that you actually have a pretty good chance to make it. It depends on a lot of variables— from how good your concept is to how much time and energy you are prepared to invest. (Writing talent surprisingly runs a poor third.) But, given all of these factors, your chances of successfully syndicating a regular column are about 50-50. We kid you not!

That's what this book is all about—how to produce and successfully sell a syndicated column. We don't guarantee a winner every time, but we can say with assurance that if you follow our guidelines, you will at least narrow the odds as much as possible, while at the same time saving yourself a lot of wheel spinning and unnecessary leg work.

HOW TO SYNDICATE YOUR OWN NEWSPAPER COLUMN

Part 1

Developing your column

Why syndicate?

A column may appear in the same newspaper as hard news stories, news features, "feature" features, editorials, reviews, and so-called think pieces. It can have elements of all of these types of articles, but it nonetheless remains a separate and distinct genre of editorial copy.

What makes a column a column is that (a) it is always written by the same author (with rare exceptions, such as when the columnist is on vacation or sick); (b) it almost always carries a "standing head" which is immediately identifiable to regular readers; (c) it appears on a regular schedule (daily, weekly, on alternate days, etc.); and (d) it carries the imprimatur or special mark of its creator.

It is an unwritten rule that columnists, like editorial writers, are free to opinionate and pontificate at will, whereas the staff reporter or freelance writer must maintain an objective approach, unless the editor gives the go-ahead for an interpretive story (in which case, it should carry such a designation in bold type).

The freedom to sound off, to accuse, to belittle, to congratulate, to salute, sets the columnist apart from all other journalists—even the editorial writers, because they simply espouse the position of the publisher instead of their own. When it comes to the "power of the press," the columnist is the single most potent individual in the fourth estate, partly because of his freedom as a writer, and partly because many more people read his column than read the usually staid editorial page.

As a result, columnists are generally the best known and most easily recognizable writers on a newspaper, especially since their pictures usually appear in the standing head of their column, or regularly appear as a head shot in the body of the column. In fact, this power and recognition (which can be rephrased as *status maximus*) is the most compelling reason so many struggling writers hanker for their own column. Becoming a columnist, especially a *syndicated* columnist, is the ultimate ego trip for a journalist or freelance writer.

Syndicates are in the business of selling editorial material (usually regularly appearing columns) to newspaper publishers, large and small. Syndicated columns are found in small town weekly newspapers, major metropolitan daily papers, including the vaunted *New York Times* and *Washington Post*. Many syndicated columnists (especially political pundits) got their start writing for a single large paper and still use it as a "base of operations."

For example, the late Walter Winchell, got his start in writing by producing a weekly gossip sheet which was pinned to the call board of a vaudeville theater in New York City (Winchell was a singer and dancer). His "column" caught the eye of the publisher of the *Vaudeville News* and Winchell was offered a reporting job at $25 a week and his first column was entitled "Stage Whispers." Winchell moved on to the *New York Graphic*, a daily with a wide readership, which operated its own syndicate and sold Winchell's show biz columns across the country.

In those days, the major dailies didn't have to compete with

TV for presenting the news, and the daily newspaper was a good deal more influential than it is today.

In Winchell's case, he recognized the power of his medium and soon began to expand his coverage to include everything from religion to politics, and with the advent of his daily radio "columns," it was said that Walter Winchell was the single most powerful individual in America. He was wooed by everyone from "Legs" Diamond (New York's most notorious gangster) to President F.D.R. himself, and in the 1930s, when he began his regular attacks on Hitler and the Nazis, the Huns labeled him their No. 1 enemy in the U.S.A.

Winchell's home base was New York City, and although he switched papers several times, he always was on the payroll of one of Gotham's major dailies until his retirement. Over the years he always regarded himself as a newspaper columnist rather than a celebrity.

While working for a single paper that eventually syndicates your column for you is one way to do it, it actually is not the best way. There are literally thousands of regular columnists on papers across the country and no more than a handful will ever see their columns syndicated. You are much better off to develop a concept for a column and then sell the idea to an established feature syndicate which will sell it for you. Or sell your column directly, acting, in effect, as your own syndicate. But more about the way to do either later.

Right now, we are going to concentrate on the most obvious ingredient for your syndicated column—the column itself, from concept to completion. Without it, you obviously can't go about the business of selling it.

And speaking of selling your column, you will be happy to learn that in a field that is notorious for low pay and rotten hours, the syndicated columnist stands apart, usually working as he pleases, and sometimes pulling down an annual income in six figures!

If that doesn't give you the incentive to read on, perhaps you should check your pulse to be sure you are still alive and kicking.

2

Subject matter

Picking a subject or area of interest for your column may sound simple, but to do it right requires a good deal of time and a lot of thought. That's because the choice of subject matter will be one of the keys to the ultimate success or failure of your column.

The days of the Walter Winchells and the Will Rogerses are pretty much gone; that is, unless you are already a nationally known figure. For example, if Howard Cosell were to write a column, he could pretty much ramble at will, not limiting himself to the sports arena, and his column would still be read. Cosell is well known and controversial, and that combination, plus his ability to use language as a violinist uses music, would spell success—at least temporarily. Whether or not the public would continue to read Cosell's commentary week after week is debatable. But that's not the point. The point is that Howard Cosell simply serves as an example of the exception to the rule about essential ingredients for the successful syndicated column.

For 99.9 percent of the rest of us, we'd never sell the idea of a rambling "general interest" column to a syndicate, or on our own to editors of papers, regardless of how well we write.

The kind of column an editor wants today is the special interest column, because that is the kind of column which will help him build readership. Newspapers have lost the battle of reporting breaking news to television, and, to a lesser extent, to radio. The one way the daily or weekly newspaper can beat the electronic media is through in-depth coverage of current news and through presenting news and information about a wide variety of subjects not covered by the radio and TV news crews.

Radio and television news shows are limited because in a full half-hour they can just about get in the equivalent of the news carried on the front page of a typical newspaper. And although they do schedule occasional specials and documentaries, the percentage is so small that it can't begin to match the volume of information in an average newspaper. This is where newspapers have the edge. Smart editors know what their readership is interested in, thanks to regular surveys conducted by the circulation and ad departments. And they do their best to make sure each issue of their paper carries as much of this material as possible.

For example, it's a pretty good bet that a community newspaper in Wausau, Wis., or Menominee, Mich., would be interested in reviewing a syndicated column on snowmobiling or skiing. Likewise, papers on both coasts and in the Great Lakes region would want to look over a column on yacht racing, whereas a paper in Kansas or Nevada would obviously not have enough reader interest to even consider such a column.

Newspapers don't just assign their own staffers to write such special-interest columns. Most newspapers are short staffed (even the biggies in places such as Chicago and New York). That means their reporters are kept hopping in covering day-to-day happenings and events. Some local staffers find the time to knock out a column now and then, and some of the major papers do carry their own "star" columnists. But there is no way that any of them can possibly begin to provide strong columns on the wide range of subjects of interest to readers. Besides, imagine the cost of creating a wide range of columns from scratch as opposed to buying similar columns from syndicates for a fraction of the cost.

The syndicates are able to sell columns for as little as a few dollars each because that same column may also be sold to a thousand other papers in other regions. As long as the column isn't sold to a competing paper in the same circulation area, no one objects. Meanwhile, the columnist can make as much as $1,000 or more for each column and so can the syndicate, while the paper gets a strong circulation booster for a few dollars. In some cases, the column material is so highly specialized or technical in nature that it would be nearly impossible for the local newspaper to duplicate it at any cost. And so, the syndicated column fills a vital need for today's newspapers.

The key to developing a successful concept for a syndicated column is to study the market thoroughly to determine what fields are overflowing with competing columns and what fields have room for more. Of course, the surest way of all to guarantee success is to find an area which virtually no one is writing about but which has enough broad appeal to be sold on a fairly large scale.

Quite frankly, there is no easy way to determine this. Your best bets are the following:

1. Check out the current volumes of the *Readers' Guide to Periodical Literature* at your local library. Look under every possible subject heading which relates to your particular area of interest and if you run across what looks like a column, find it and see for yourself.

2. While you are at the library (assuming it is in a major city), take an afternoon and skim the issues of the various major city newspapers that your library carries. Or go to the newsstand in your city that carries out-of-town papers and buy one of each to study.

3. Call 15 or 20 newspapers (both daily and weekly) in your

region and ask the editors if a column or your area of interest is available now and, if not, would they consider taking one on should it become available?

4. Send $3 for a current copy of the *Editor & Publisher Syndicate Directory* (*E & P* is the trade paper of the newspaper industry) to E & P, 575 Lexington Ave., New York, N.Y. 10022. Or use our own list of major feature syndicates which appears at the end of this chapter.

With directory in hand, you can either write queries to various editors (syndicates are classified according to subject matter), or send a form letter to them all, asking for a list of the columns they offer.

If you do this, your next step will be to check carefully your column idea against each of the lists, This will avoid the time and trouble of preparing sample columns, only to discover upon submitting them that something identical is already available. Besides, if you submit samples of a column on basket weaving this month and don't sell it, and then come back next month with sample columns on scuba diving, the editors are likely to remember you and label you as just another hustler.

Your chances of selling a concept to a syndicate will be enhanced if you pick a subject about which you know a great deal and can list credentials to prove it.

For example, suppose you played soccer in high school and college and then went on to coach a pro team. Obviously, you are in a position to talk about the sport in an expert way, providing, of course, that you are also able to write in an interesting and understandable manner.

Or, suppose your hobby is buying old houses, fixing them up, and then reselling them at a profit. Who would be in a better position to write a column on home repairs and remodeling?

These are the kind of things a syndicate loves to see in your background because they are able to use them in their own promotional literature to help sell your column to newspapers.

A good way to come up with general ideas for columns is to look over your own job resume. Then ask some of your friends to join you for a "think tank" session, where everyone tries to come up with ideas for you. Then, with idea list in hand, you can follow up by checking each out as outlined above.

One way to get everyone thinking in the right vein is to use the following list of topic ideas as "teasers":

Accidents: This topic could be approached from many angles—how to avoid them, first aid treatment, etc.

Agriculture: This could range from "how to" ideas for home gardeners to various news and information of interest to full-time farmers.

Animals: The possibilities are almost endless: caring for pets; animal anecdotes; habits of animals; or how to recognize breeds.

Architecture: If you are an architect or home builder, this would be a natural. You could describe interesting and unusual homes, and include photos or sketches.

Armed forces: News of interest to servicemen and/or their families might seem far-fetched, but think of how many towns have military bases in or near them and thus have a high percentage of service personnel as readers.

Arms: With more than a million members of the National Riflemen's Association and upwards of 60 million hunters in the country, a column on sporting guns has plenty of possibilities.

Art: This could range from a series of columns devoted to major artists, to discussions on various areas of art appreciation, collecting, etc.

Astronomy: With the space age in full swing, and the talk of strange encounters and UFOs flying about, the time appears ripe for an intelligent syndicated column on astronomy. And, of course, the material is endless (no pun intended).

Authors: This could be reviews of books, blurbs on upcoming works, or even biographical sketches.

Automation: With the age of computers upon us, the material for columns is vast.

Automobiles: There are already plenty of automobile columns, not to mention the abundance of enthusiast magazines, but such a vast area of interest is bound to have possibilities for new angles.

Aviation: You might produce vignettes on special events in aviation history. Or how about a column on small planes?

Babies: Come up with a fresh angle and you could become another Dr. Spock.

Bachelor life: With more and more people remaining single or getting divorced, a column for bachelors, bachelorettes, or singles in general, has all kinds of possibilities.

Baseball: Good luck on this one. It's been worked to death.

Bible: With being "born again" in vogue these days, the possibilities for a column on Bible study, or application of Bible teaching to everyday life, are many. The trick, of course, is to be able to write so that you don't bump heads with various opposing views.

Bicycling: Here's one of the hottest new crazes, and it looks as if it will not be fading away. Possibilities range from general tips to repair information.

Bird watching: As interest in ecology grows, so does the interest in just watching as opposed to hunting.

Blind people: If you can come up with a column filled with news and ideas for the sightless, you could probably sell a regular column to many papers which would view such a column as a public service.

Books: Although columns are available dealing with reviews of new books, there are still a lot of possibilities for dealing with books, from listing interesting new releases, to discussing the classics.

Boy scouting: Why not? Every community has Cub Scouts, Boy Scouts, Girl Scouts, Explorer Scouts. A column dealing with various aspects of scouting might appeal both to scouts and parents.

Bridge: Forget it. There are already too many Bridge columns.

Business: Columns on business could include success stories of small and large businesses, tax tips, or be a roundup of news. Smaller papers especially need help in this area, since few have their own business writer.

Carpentry: How about a how-to column, complete with photos or illustrations, for the do-it-yourselfers?

Celebrities: The public never seems to get too much information about celebrities of all types. Find a different angle (plus a way to get information until you establish yourself like Rona and Rex) and you'll sell your column.

Child care: *See* Babies.

Children: Almost every adult is a parent, so if you can develop an angle for talking about kids which hasn't been used yet, you'll have a potential winner.

Christmas: Yes, there *is* a market for columns on Christmas, albeit seasonal. But why not a column that covers each holiday as it approaches?

Church: Possibilities include new developments, differences in beliefs, history of famous or unusual churches, etc.

Clothes: Different from fashion columns, since you could discuss functional clothes, how to clean them, new ideas in clothes, fabrics, and so on.

Clubs: With literally thousands of social, fraternal, civic, business, religious, and other clubs, possibilities for a column are limitless.

Coffee: Sounds crazy, but when you consider the number of people who drink coffee, the many kinds available and the endless ways of preparing coffee, the subject has possibilities.

Coins: Coin collecting is a hobby with a surprisingly large following. Not only that, just think if you discussed a single valuable coin in each column which the average person just might have on his person? Instant lottery time!

College: With several thousand institutions of higher learning, column possibilities boggle the mind.

Conservation: The time is ripe for such columns.

Contests: With countless contests underway every day, you could simply advise people about good ones and tell how to enter.

Corporations: Columns could range from discussing individual corporations to problems facing corporations.

Crafts: If you know enough about a "hot" one such as macrame to write intelligently about it, you're bound to sell your concept.

Crime: Possibilities include methods of prevention, recounting "famous" crimes, and defining various crimes.

Dancing: Thanks to *Saturday Night Fever,* plus the boom in disco dancing, you'll be seeing a lot of dance columns popping up.

Dating: Find a way to reach the teen-age audience and you've got a winner.

Dentistry: History, discussion of dental problems, etc.

Divorce: With 50 percent of the adult population eventually facing divorce, the possibilities for columns are many.

Dogs: Everyone loves dogs, so just find a new angle.

Do-it-yourself: Plenty of possibilities.

Drama: Culture is in vogue, so drama has possibilities.

Dreams: Who isn't curious about dreams? Of course, it might help in writing this type of column if your name is Sigmund.

Driving: Almost everyone drives, so you can offer tips, discuss safety, etc.

Drugs: This column could be devoted to drug abuse, or it could include descriptions of readily available drugs for the medicine chest.

Eating: Could range from discussions of new diets (it seems like a new one comes along each day), to unusual dishes.

Education: Talk to a teacher for possibilities here.

Electronics: How about new electronic devices?

Employment: Ideas for getting jobs; fields that have good employment possibilities; news of available benefits, and so on.

Evangelism: Great possibilities in the Bible Belt.

Farming: *See* Agriculture.

Fathers: There are a whole lot of fathers out there. Why not a column just for them?

Films: *See* Books.

Finance: The column could range from information on obtaining loans and mortgages, to handling the home budget.

Fishing: There is always room for unusual approaches to the most popular of all participant sports.

Flowers: Possibilities include growing them, identifying wild flowers, and flower arranging.

Folklore: If you told a tale a day, you'd never run out of ideas.

Foods: Possibilities range from shopping tips to identifying edible wild foods.

Football: Forget it.

Fruit: *See* Foods.

Furniture: Ideas include buying, repairing, and collecting.

Games: Possibilities are almost endless.

Gifts: How about zeroing in on an unusual gift possibility each day. The column could range from the sublime to the ridiculous.

Golf: Forget instruction—it's overworked. But how about a brief history, comments on famous courses, or biographies of famous golfers?

Gossip: The gossip column is back in all its glory. But to do a syndicated column, you have to have plenty of connections for inside information.

Government: Apathy has turned to antagonism. How about a column advising how to deal with government bureaucracy?

Happiness: Everyone wants it. Tell 'em how to find it.

Health: Ditto.

Heroes: Biographical sketches, or maybe the "real" story of men like Custer, Jesse James, etc.

History: Really make it interesting, and it could sell.

Hobbies: Good lord!

Homes: *See* Architecture.

Homosexuality: With gays popping up all over the place, who knows? There just might be a market for a gay column.

Horses: *See* Dogs.

Hunting: *See* Fishing.

Illness: *See* Health.

Income: How about ideas for extra income?

Inflation: Talk about a timely topic. How to beat it is a natural.

Insurance: If you are knowledgeable, you could certainly come up with enough material for a regular column.

Intelligence: How about mini-I. Q. tests?

Jobs: *See* Employment.

Labor: A column aimed at the blue collar class could be successful.

Law: Ideas range from discussions of quaint and outdated laws to dealing with today's myriad of local, state, and federal laws.

Literature: *See* Books.

Marriage: Endless possibilities.

Medicine: *See* Drugs.

Motorcycles: With the gas crunch on for the foreseeable future, motorcycles are "in."

Music: Most papers have a music critic, but there's still plenty to say about this subject, if you are knowledgeable.

Names: What's in a name? Why not tell 'em?

Negroes: Black people want recognition. A syndicated column could help give it to them, *and* you.

Opera: Why not?

Palmistry: Interest in the occult is there. So if you can come up with a humorous or really unusual treatment of palmistry, numerology, witchcraft, devil worship, etc., you might be able to sell it.

Patents: Just mentioning the kookiest would give you enough material for years.

Pets: *See* Animals; dogs.

Photography: Interest in it is growing by the day.

Plants: Ditto.

Poetry: Who knows? It might fly.

Politics: About the same chance as Baseball.

Psychiatry: If Dr. Joyce Brothers can make a living writing and talking about it, why can't you?

Railroads: If you know enough about railroads, you might be able to develop a column that would appeal to the millions of buffs out in the hinterlands.

Real estate: With property values rising faster than Mom's bread, any new approach to this hot topic will sell—fast!

Records: If you can write like a teeny bopper and you can tell Queen from Abba, you've got it knocked.

Recreation: Possibilities range from vacation trip ideas to participant sports and hobbies.

Religion: *See* Church.

Restaurants: A syndicated column on restaurants? Why not? Pick a top restaurant in a major city or vacation area for each column, for example.

Science: Make science fun and understandable for the masses and the column could go.

Sports: Know enough about one of the new "boom" sports such as skateboarding, cycling, and jogging to write intelligently about it? Then you'll probably be able to sell your column. But forget about such overworked sports as tennis and skiing. (An exception for skiing would be a travel-oriented column, highlighting individual ski resorts rather than dealing with "how to do it.")

Solar power: There is certainly enough interest in solar energy. The question is, can you come up with enough to say on a continuing basis to justify a regular column?

Taxes: One of the two "sure things," as the old saw goes. So if you know your stuff and can make this subject interesting, you've got a winner.

Television: Yes, there are a lot of television writers, but if you really have a novel idea for talking about the boob tube, it will sell.

Toys: Possible angles include far-out and novel toys, ripoffs, toy safety, etc.

Travel: Once again, here is an overworked subject that could still be used if you had a unique approach.

Vacations: Ditto.

Wearing apparel: Could include fashions, tips on buying clothes, etc.

Weather: Impossible to do a forecast column, that is, unless you do something different, such as forecasting by the activities of fish and animals or providing forecasts for the coming week or month on a nationwide scale.

Weight control: *See* Dieting.

Women: Possibilities include women's lib (including the chauvinist's viewpoint), special problems of women (health, employment, etc.), and special news of interest to women.

Obviously, this list was not meant to be all-inclusive. But it should give you an idea of how to go about developing topics for a syndicated column.

Partial list of major feature syndicates

American Features Syndicate, 964 Third Ave., New York, N.Y. 10022. Will consider travel series, but not regular, ongoing columns. Pays up to $750. Write to David Mark, editor.

Authenticated News International, 170 Fifth Ave., New York, N.Y. 10010. Specializes in human interest, travel, animals, science. Pays 50 percent royalty. Write to Jesse Seigel, editor.

Chicago Tribune/New York News Syndicate, 220 E. 42nd St., New York, N.Y. 10017. Interested in politics, women, humor, sports, health, food, furnishings, fashion. Pays 50 percent royalty with contract. Submit at least six sample columns, plus statement of philosophy. Send to Thomas Dorsey, editor.

General Features, Times Mirror Square, Los Angeles, Calif. 90053. Interested in columns and feature series. Payment is by contract arrangement. Write to Pat McHugh, chief editor.

Dave Goodwin & Associates, Box 6094, Surfside, Fla. 33154. Buys column ideas as well as non-fiction consumer-oriented features to 500 words. Write to Dave Goodwin, editor.

Greenwich Features, Inc., Time-Life Building, New York, N.Y. 10020. Looking for 5- to 10-part features on special subjects and well-documented columns on all subjects. Payment negotiable. Contact George Foley, executive editor.

King Features Syndicate, 235 E. 45th St., New York, N.Y. 10017. Interested in column ideas and features on most nonfiction subjects, including service material and leisure time activities. Columns paid through contract arrangement. Prefer 500 to 700 words per column. Write to Neal Freeman, editor.

Los Angeles Times Syndicate, Times Mirror Square, Los Angeles, Calif. 90053. Buys columns on all subjects with payment through contract. Also purchases individual features. Write to Patrick McHugh, editor.

McNaught Syndicate, Inc., 60 E. 42nd St., New York 10017. Looking for columns dealing with humor, politics (especially the Washington scene), and medical subjects. Contracts offered for continuing columns. Write to Anne Rickey, editor.

Mel Martin Enterprises, Box 22505, Houston, Tex. 77027. Interested in cmlumns and feature articles on adventure, boating, business, investments, and cars (including racing). Pays up to 40 percent of selling price. Write to Mel Martin Jr., editor.

Mid-Continent Feature Syndicate, Box 1662, Pittsburgh, Pa. 15230. Interested in syndicated columns on drama, fashion, food, business, humor, and book reviews. Also buys serialization rights for books, and individual features. Write to Charles Conover, editorial chairman.

National Catholic News Service, 1312 Massachusetts Ave., N.W., Washington, D.C. 20005. Looking for columns on everything from labor and business to liturgy. Also purchases news and feature stories. Contracts available for continuing columns, and 5¢ per word for individual features. Write to A.E.P. Wall, editor.

National Feature Syndicate, 1052-A National Press Building, Washington, D.C. 20004. Wants column ideas and individual features on political aspects of health and insurance industries. Write to Fred Rosenblatt, editor.

National Newspaper Syndicate, 20 N. Wacker Dr., Chicago, Ill. 60606. Strictly looking for continuing columns on specific subjects. Write to Tom Hirsh, editor.

NC News Service, *see* **National Catholic News Service.**

Newsco Press Features, Inc., Box 91, Blairsville, Pa. 15717. Looking for columns and individual pieces on sports, especially with a nostalgia angle. Contracts offered for columns. Articles sought up to 2,000 words, with payment up to $150. Write to William Thomas, editor.

Newspaper Enterprise Assn., 230 Park Ave., New York 10017. Looking for both columns and single features, especially carefully researched science pieces. Contracts offered for columns, and payment to $500 for features. Write to Robert Cochnar, editor.

North American Newspaper Alliance, 220 E. 42nd St., New York 10017. Mostly interested in feature ideas, but will consider outstanding columns. Supplies materials to papers worldwide. Payment negotiable. Write to Sheldon Engelmayer, editor.

Numismatic Information Service, Rossway Road, Pleasant Valley, N.Y. 12569. Buys individual features and column ideas on coin collecting. Pays $5 per column per week; maximum length—500 words. Write to Barbara White, editor.

Oceanic Press Service, 4717 Laurel Canyon Blvd., North Hollywood, Calif. 91607. Pays 50 percent royalties on columns and serialized features on crime-stopping, extrasensory perception (ESP), "quickie" mystery solutions, "test yourself" features, etc. Write to J. Taylor, editor.

Publishers-Hall Syndicate, 401 N. Wabash Ave., Chicago 60611. Looking for top column ideas. (This organization syndicates such columnists as Ann Landers, Joseph Kraft, Sylvia Porter, and Erma Bombeck.) Especially interested in service and "do-it-yourself" columns. Payment according to newspaper sales. Write to Richard Sherry, editor.

Register & Tribune Syndicate, 715 Locust St., Des Moines, Ia. 50304. Buys feature series and columns on subjects of current interest, such as the environment, women's lib, etc. (This organization syndicates such columns as "The Better Half" and "The Family Circus.") Payment through royalty commission. Write to Dennis Allen, president.

Trans-World News Service, Box 2801, Washington, D.C. 20013. Buys continuing columns and features on international travel, business, etc. Also interested in entertainment and columns for women. Pays $5 to $100 per feature or column. Write to E. Rothkirch, editor.

United Feature Syndicate, Inc., 220 E. 42nd St., New York 10017. Looking for feature series (3 to 6 parts), and column ideas on do-it-yourself, personalities, and human interest subjects. (Columnists include Jack Anderson, William S. White, and Barbara Gibbons.) Pays 50 percent commission. Write to James Freeman, managing editor.

U.S. News Service, Room 862, National Press Building, Washington, D.C. 20004. Buys features and column ideas dealing with humor, poetry, and general interest. Payment negotiable. Write to Walter Fisk, bureau chief.

Douglas Whiting, Ltd., 930 De Courcelle St., Montreal, P.Q., Canada. Looking for features and continuing columns dealing with science, puzzles and contests. Write to D.P. Whiting, editor.

Women's News Service, 220 E. 42nd St., New York, N.Y. 10017. Mainly interested in single features and series, but will occasionally consider an outstanding idea for a continuing column. Any subject of special interest to women. Minimum payment is $25 but can go much higher. Write to Sid Goldberg, editor.

Zodiac News Service, 950 Howard St., San Francisco, Calif. 94103. Interested in feature and column ideas for use by FM stations across the United States. Payment negotiable. Write to Jon Newhall, editor.

3

Developing your column idea

At this point, you have completed the laborious, but basically simple task of compiling a working list of potential subjects for your column. You have talked with friends, cross-checked all the column listings you were able to get your hands on to avoid duplication, and talked to a number of area newspaper editors as well.

Your "potential column subject list" should be boiled down to a dozen or fewer items. The next step is to rearrange them in order of importance. Rather than just going at this task in a haphazard manner, I suggest you evaluate each column idea by the three following criteria, giving the same number of points as column ideas to the first choice, one point less to the second choice, and so on:

1. Your own knowledge of the subject matter
2. Interest of the public in the subject matter
3. Potential for "continuous input"

The first of these, knowledge of the subject matter, should be an obvious essential ingredient for a column choice, even if that knowledge is easily learned. In order to write intelligently about a subject, you should be totally comfortable with it. Otherwise, you will find yourself struggling to comprehend its jargon and then to translate "shop language" so your readers can also understand it. Knowledge of the subject matter also implies that you have contacts who will make themselves available for interviews and questions and who will tip you off on inside news and gossip. Developing such contacts takes time, even for seasoned pros. That's why when an editor assigns a reporter to a new beat, he allows several months before demanding top performance. And writing a regular column is very much like covering a beat. If you think it can be done sitting at a desk, you are dead wrong.

Does that mean you should rule out any column ideas or concepts about which you aren't an expert? Of course not, but it may mean that you should spend six months to a year researching the subject and writing freelance feature articles about it before you try to sell your column idea. The time spent will not only provide you with much needed knowledge, but it will also provide you with income and credibility as an authority in the field. (Be sure to save all clippings of published work for submission with your column ideas and sample columns.)

The second of the three criteria for evaluating your column—interest of the public in the subject matter—will have a direct bearing on the ability of a syndicate to sell your column to newspapers and other publications. Ultimately, it will determine the potential earnings for you as well. So it must rank as one of the three primary yardsticks for evaluating your idea.

As for the final element, potential for "continuous input," we mean simply the likelihood that you will not run out of "ammunition" after six months or a year of grinding out your column on a daily or weekly basis. If you don't think this is worthy of worry, just talk to anyone who has ever written a column, whether it be for a club newsletter or the local paper. After a short time, what started out as a "piece of cake," turns out to be an agonizing ordeal. Many are the first-rate reporters who wangled and cajoled their bosses into letting them write a column only to crawl back later and beg to be let off the hook. The most obvious symptom of this dreaded malady is when the new columnist resorts to interviewing cronies at the newspaper, or taking strong stands on noncontroversial issues. (Watch for key phrases such as "I urge you" or "deserves a lot of credit" or "on the other hand.")

Now that we've defined the three key criteria for evaluating your column idea, here's an example of how the method works:

Suppose one of the potential column topics is real estate investing. It is one of five remaining on your list after a preliminary screening. You compare it with the others and conclude it tops the list in relation to your own knowledge of the subject matter. (Perhaps you used to work for a real estate broker, or you wrote occasional feature articles on real estate, or you invest your savings in real estate as a kind of hobby.)

In any case, since real estate investing tops the list, you give it five points. If water skiing is your second choice for knowledge of subject matter, it gets four points, and so on, with the topic you know least getting a single point.

You then go through the same process in evaluating your list as to interest of the reading public and potential for continuous input. The final step is to total the points for each of your column ideas and then rank them accordingly.

Don't discard those topics with the fewest points. Simply give them a lower priority when you begin the actual process of developing and promoting your column to syndicates. Take one topic at a time and devote your whole attention to developing and selling it.

If you strike out with the first choice, then go on to the second choice, and so on until your list is eliminated totally. If you haven't sold a column idea at this point, perhaps you should take a long, hard look at your writing before compiling a brand new list and starting all over. Some people just don't have the knack for writing a column.

If you think that perhaps you fall into this classification, your best bet for getting a realistic appraisal of your talents is to:

1. Check with one or more of your old journalism professors. If you didn't major in journalism, send a few sample columns to a reputable journalism school and ask for an appraisal. Advise that you would be willing to pay a reasonable fee to have one of the professors in the journalism department evaluate your work.

2. Send a couple of your sample columns to the local newspaper, again asking that they be evaluated and advising that you would be willing to pay one of the editors a reasonable fee to tackle the chore as a moonlighting job. Chances are you'll get the evaluation for free, especially if you live in a smaller town.

Do not ask family or friends to appraise your work. First of all, they are likely to simply tell you how good it is, even if it stinks. And second, what do they know, anyway, about the merits of writing a column?

Finally, do not sign up for one of those mail order writing courses, where they ask you to send in a sample of your work for evaluation. Naturally, they are going to encourage you in the hope that they'll get you as a customer.

What about asking the syndicates you sent your material to for an appraisal? Lots of luck! They have neither the time nor the inclination to get into the appraisal business. Besides, if they didn't buy your stuff, it is obvious they didn't like it for one reason or another.

But more on the actual process of selling your ideas later. Right now, let's get down to the next step—that of actually writing your column.

To begin with, there is no magic formula for writing a column. If there were, every single column that was written by that formula would come out sounding like every other such column, regardless of content. News stories, for example, are generally written according to a formula, and many newspapers insist on it for good reason.

The news story formula is the five Ws—who, what, where, when, and why. Some journalists will add an H to the list—how.

Unless a story has these basic ingredients, it won't get past the copy desk. And, with rare exceptions, all five Ws and the H must be in the lead paragraph.

There is method to this apparent madness. Space in most newspapers is at a premium. Stories must be compact and concise. And they must be written paragraph by paragraph in order of descending importance. The idea is that if the story is slated for a given "news hole," and it runs long, or a late ad is dumped onto a page, the story can be trimmed without losing its meaning.

That's why you will almost never see news stories written with a trick ending, or a "punch line." Such a story must run in its entirety, and as such, it will cause havoc with the makeup editor in the composing room. But the story that has all the essentials at the top can often be cut and recut and still tell its message to the reader.

The formula rule applies equally to important page one stories as well as the small items buried on page 36 or elsewhere in the paper. The exceptions to this rule are editorials, feature stories, "think" pieces, and columns.

To avoid problems with getting such stories to fit the news hole, they are almost always dummied onto pages which are open (have no ads), or in a place where they will not have to be trimmed. To make sure the column or feature fits the given amount of space, the writers are usually under instructions to "give us 650 words" or "make sure that story has a photo with it that can be trimmed.

In the case of the syndicated column, it is the job of the copy editor and layout editor on the various papers to place it where it will fit in its entirety, unless it is of such a nature that it can be trimmed from the bottom or by the deletion of various paragraphs in the middle.

Of course, it goes without saying that few syndicated columnists (with the exception of major political pundits) ever have any say on how their column is handled by individual papers. Once you sell it, you lose all control over it. So if you are a prima donna about your work, you'd better stick to writing on individual assignments where you can spell out any restrictions on editing or cutting when you sell the article.

The "New" Journalism

Chances are you have run across this breed of writing in recent years, whether or not you were able to categorize it. This so-called "new" journalism is not really new at all, despite the fact that Tom Wolfe, its high priest, claims that it is the product of the 1960s.

In short, Wolfe says that the "new" journalists have taken the many literary devices formerly limited to use by novelists and adopted them for reporting news events. While he is correct, he fails to take into account that the use of literary techniques by journalists has been going on ever since the invention of the printing press. The colonial firebrand Tom Paine is a perfect example, as was the writing of Ben Franklin to a lesser extent. Then there was Mark Twain, whose work for newspapers was not unlike his "more serious" writing efforts.

And, closer to our own time, the best example of a journalist using literary technique is Ernest Hemingway, whose news stories were actually short stories. They were the vehicles which actually helped Hemingway develop his staccato, machine gun style. Proof of the literary merit of his various news dispatches while a reporter in Kansas City, later in Toronto, lies in the fact that an anthology of them, entitled *By-Line: Ernest Hemingway,* was later published in book form and became a best seller.

There were others, such as war correspondent Ernie Pyle and sportswriter Red Smith, both of whom strayed far from the standard journalistic form in their writing.

Nonetheless, Tom Wolfe is correct insomuch as the so-called new journalism came to full flower in the 1960s and 1970s, with such writers as Truman Capote, Terry Southern, George Plimpton, Hunter Thompson, and Gay Talese. What he does not elaborate on is that almost all of the "new" journalism appears in magazines rather than newspapers, and no wonder. Where the average news story must be kept to a few hundred words (the bombing of Pearl Harbor was reported by the *Chicago American* in 350 words), the "new" journalists, in adopting the format of the short story and novellette, locked themselves into pieces of several thousand words at the least.

As any cub reporter will tell you, anyone can cover a village board meeting, at which 14 different items are on the agenda, and come away with a story that runs to 10 or 15 typed pages. It takes a pro to boil that meeting down to a digestible two typed pages (double spaced, of course). As Wolfe admitted in his own book on the New Journalism, the last story he ever wrote that was held to 1,500 words (*1,500 words!*) was a feature about demolition derbies on Long Island. "After that, they started climbing to 3,000, 4,000, 5,000, 6,000 words. Like Pascal, I was sorry, but I didn't have the time to write short ones," he confessed.

Frankly, we enjoy much of what has been labeled "new" journalism. Stories such as Richard Goldstein's "Gear," one of a series on the Vietnam War that appeared in the *Village Voice,* and "Beth Ann and Macrobioticism" by Robert Christgau that appeared in 1966 in the *New York Herald Tribune,* grip you and virtually demand that you read them all the way to the finish.

We don't even object to some of the devices created by the "new" journalists to grab the reader's attention—mannerisms such as the lavish use of dots, dashes, exclamation points, bold face, italics, different size type, even newly invented uses of punctuation::::::::::::. The "new" journalists make up their own words, often combining various other words; they use poetic devices such as onomatopoeia.

But, let's face it. The "new" journalism is simply not adaptable to the rigid limitations of space placed on most columnists, especially syndicated ones. Most papers don't want to talk to a syndicate about a column unless it is "short and sweet." Columns from 300 to 500 words are par for the course, and seldom will you ever see columns of more than 1,000 words being sold successfully by a syndicate (unless it is written by the likes of

Bert Lance, former President Gerald Ford, or some other well-known personality.)

Keep it short

Those three words have been issued by more editors than perhaps any other instructions to reporters and columnists. The "news hole" of virtually every newspaper has been shrinking in reverse proportion to the cost of production. Every time a price hike is announced in the per ton cost of newsprint, the percentage of advertising to editorial material in the paper changes.

Not too long ago, most papers ran 20 percent or 25 percent advertising and devoted the bulk of their space to stories, columns, photos, and other editorial matter. But the pendulum has been swinging inexorably, so that many newspapers today have a hard time keeping the advertising to editorial ratio at 75/25 in order to qualify for second-class mailing permits under U.S. Postal Service regulations.

It's a case of either cutting down on the percentage of news to advertising (in other words, cutting down on pages) or raising ad rates. Since papers have found that when they raise ad rates, they invariably lose some advertisers, the choice is usually to reduce the news hole instead.

In order to get as many stories, photos, columns, and editorials in as before, everyone feels the space crunch. And since columns are considered nonessential material, they are often hit the hardest.

So, when you set about the task of selling your idea for a column, and you write three or four sample columns, keep them short. It will let the editor of the syndicate know that you can write within tight confines. Chances are that when you do sign a contract, it will include the stipulation that your columns be held to a given number of words.

4

Writing the column

The purpose of this book is not to teach you how to write. We assume that this is one skill you already have. It doesn't matter so much whether you have actual experience as a working journalist (in other words, been on the payroll of a newspaper), or you have been freelancing, or even that your writing has been limited to unpublished efforts. What matters is that you have the confidence and the ability to write in an interesting manner while getting your message across within the confines of space allowed.

Of course, if you've never done any writing at all, the place to start is *not* with a column, syndicated or otherwise. You should start by taking a few writing courses, or at the very least by reading several "how to" books on writing. Follow that up by writing *and* selling a dozen or more individual pieces to newspapers and magazines. When you get to this point, you will have the confidence and ability to try selling your column ideas.

Taking the preliminary steps first will require a year or two, but it will greatly increase your odds of selling your column idea.

Tricks of the trade

Although writing a column is not the same as writing a hard news story, a feature article, or an editorial, the columnist is free to use devices common to all of these as well as any others he feels will help him make his point.

1. Narrow down your subject. Granted, your column has already narrowed down your subject matter, but we are talking about the highly specific area of concern for today's or this week's column. If you are to stay within your limit of words, you must confine your discussion to as confined a subject matter as possible. For example, if your column is about stamp collecting, your topic should be something such as "The New 15-Cent 1st-Class Stamp." If your column deals with home improvement, your topic should be something such as "How to Tack Down Carpeting" or "Hanging Pictures."

2. Pinpoint exactly what you want to accomplish in the column. Maybe your objective is to simply relate a human-interest story designed to grab the reader by the heartstrings. Or you may be issuing a warning, making a prediction, or capturing a glimpse of a particular person's unique personality. It is essential that you figure out exactly what your goal for this particular column is so that you can zero in on it without any deviation. That means getting right down to the bare facts. Columnists can rarely afford the luxury of detailed description or flowing narrative. In this respect, you must function exactly as the hard news reporter. If names, dates, places, times are necessary to accomplish the goal of this particular column, then these facts must be included.

3. Make an outline. Sounds too elementary, doesn't it? But the best journalists always work with an outline except when they are writing the most basic news story. The outline will keep

you right on track and will insure that you don't waste any words getting right to the point.

4. Use quotes sparingly. Quotes can be a most effective tool for making a point, but the neophyte writer tends to use them as crutches. He often starts his story or column with a quote. He also tends to rely on the quote to "wrap up" his column. And when in a bind in the body of the piece, he falls back on the quote. This is not to say that you should never start or end a story with a quote or that you should never use a lot of quotes in a given column. Never say "never" when it comes to establishing rules of writing. Any rule can be bent or broken to great effect, but only if you know exactly what point you are trying to make. In general, the more quotes you use in a given column, the weaker each individual quote becomes. As the old saw goes, too much of a good thing can ruin it. And that bit of paraphrasing is a way to capture the essence of a quotation without resorting to the use of quotation marks. Just remember that if you do paraphrase something that belongs to a specific individual, always attribute it to that person.

5. Use the dictionary and *Roget's Thesaurus*. The rule of the copy desk is, "When in doubt, look it up." The rule applies especially to the columnist since you are considered an expert in your particular subject area. Use a word in not exactly the right way and you lose credibility with your readers. Don't count on a copy editor in Dubuque to correct your misspellings and incorrect use of words. Often, the syndicated column gets short shrift in the local newsroom as deadline pressures require that local stories get most careful scrutiny.

Use the dictionary to check spelling and to make sure of any words you are not totally sure about. This is just as important after you syndicate your column as when you are still trying to sell the concept. If you get a reputation as a hack, it will be only a matter of time before your column goes under, and then you will have to live with a bad reputation as a writer as well.

The thesaurus is an equally valuable tool, and, rest assured, every successful author and journalist uses one. It enables you to come up with just the right choice of words when two or more could be used. And it helps to prevent the overuse of the same hackneyed verbs which lend themselves to particular subjects.

6. Develop a "Slang" list. If you are writing a column about a subject matter that lends itself to specific technical language or jargon, develop a working list so that you are able to communicate effectively with your readers. If, for example, your column deals with automobile racing, you ought to be using words such as "understeer," "pushing in the corners," "fast time," and other jargon familiar to drivers and fans alike. If you are writing a column on skiing, don't be afraid to use words such as "sitzmark," "schuss," "slalom," "skiing the crud," and similar jargon.

The trick is to write in such a way that a layman will be able to grasp the general meaning of what you say, while the enthusiast feels as if you are talking just to him.

7. Include the reader by addressing him. That means using the second person, you, as frequently as possible. This can be accomplished by directly addressing the reader, or by indirect means, such as is the case in this paragraph.

8. Be careful of cliches. One of the first things the cub reporter is warned about is the use of cliches. But it's easier said than done. (See what we mean?) Even old timers catch themselves occasionally falling into the cliche trap. Why avoid cliches? Because they make your writing sound hackneyed, worn out, ordinary. Just remember that there is a distinct difference between a cliche and a figure of speech. The figure of speech can vividly drive home an impression without the drawbacks of a cliche.

For example, here are two ways to say the same thing. The first example uses a cliche, while the second uses a figure of speech:

A. "She was as cool as a cucumber."
B. "She was as cool as a freshly made bed."

9. Avoid puns. While they may not be the lowest form of humor, as some claim, they do tend to force a laugh. You are much better off to understate something humorous and let it

creep up on your reader, rather than to distract him with an obvious pun.

10. Give your column a twist. That could mean building suspense, creating a problem to be dealt with, or posing a question. Regardless of which technique you use, we in the trade call this slipping the reader "the hook." It is simply using some kind of device to pull your reader right into the guts of your piece.

11. Don't overuse statistics. As everyone knows, statistics can be used to whatever end you choose. As a result, most intelligent readers become wary when they are confronted with a barrage of numbers. Like the quote, the statistic is best used sparingly. Understatement is far more effective than glaring repetition.

12. Poking fun can be dangerous. The columnist is not restrained like a reporter. He can make jibes and digs without having to back them up with facts or proof. But that doesn't mean it is the right thing to do. Use your discretion in firing barbs. Taking a cheap shot, or hitting below the belt, usually results in a backlash among your readers. People have a tendency to rally with the underdog. Better to make your case and let the reader come to the conclusion on his own (or at least let him think he comes to the conclusion on his own).

13. Keep your paragraphs short. Here is another old newspaper axiom. but we advise it for a different reason. Newspapers want short paragraphs so that if they have to trim, they can do it in small increments. But we favor the short paragraph because it adds "punch" and vitality to your writing, especially when you are limited for space.

14. Don't regionalize. If your column is syndicated, that means it is reaching people all across the country, and possibly elsewhere, too. Don't let yourself write to a particular audience, and don't pick a topic that will not have any interest for people outside a given region. You can relate a story about a specific place or person, but be sure you do it in a way that others can relate to. Perhaps you single out an unwed mother in Oklahoma City. What is it about her situation that is the same as unwed mothers in Chicago or Boston?

15. Humor can be deadly. Make no mistake about it—

humorous writing is the most difficult of all, at least if it is done right. You are better off trying to write a serious piece which turns out funny than attempting a side splitter which falls on its face.

16. "You are there!" Edward R. Murrow used this technique to maximum effectiveness in his broadcasts. It can also be applied to the written word, and when done properly, can produce incredible impact. Best of all, this technique works for all kinds of occasions and events, from the most grim (an execution) to the frivolous (the annual Easter pilgrimage of students to Florida beaches).

17. Repeat for impact. Pick the key word in your account and hammer it home. For example:

"All right, you poor excuses for Marines. Fix bayonets. Now charge those dummies. Parry! Thrust! Kill! Kill! Kill!!!"

These two sentences put you right in the middle of a Marine boot camp, with the D.I. shouting to the recruits on the bayonet practice field. And they did it without so much as an introduction. In fact, this could very well function as an introduction to a column on the rigors of basic training, or the brutality inherent in becoming a Marine.

The interview

Although it could simply be listed as No. 18 in a list of devices and techniques to be employed by the columnist, it is of such import that it deserves special attention.

Interviewing people is an art and a science at the same time. It requires insight, concentration, understanding, and, above all, the ability to break through the barriers set up by the interviewee.

Interviews are handled in myriad ways by journalists. No one way is right or wrong. Some people meticulously prepare a list of questions to be asked. Others simply let the interviewee start to talk and allow the interview to take whatever direction it drifts in. Still others carefully manipulate the interviewee without the appearance of doing so.

Some writers use a tape recorder. Others use a notebook. And still others simply commit the conversation to memory. Interviews can be conducted just about anywhere, too—on a plane, in a waiting room, on the playing field, in a locker room, or over dinner or drinks.

What makes some interviews click while others bomb out? We said it above—it is the interviewer's ability to break through the barriers, not the setting or the time of day, or anything else. To do this, you have to put yourself in the place of the interviewee.

Is he a controversial figure? If so, he's probably been badgered by the press and misquoted on several occasions. Chances are that he regards all writers as "the enemy," people to be avoided when possible, and when not, to be thwarted. Your best bet for beating his antagonism is by not waiting until the interview takes place. As soon as you know that you will be interviewing a particular person, write him a brief note stating that you are looking forward to meeting him. Send a few clippings of other interviews in which he comes out in a favorable light. This will help set his mind at ease.

Next, do your homework. If you are interviewing a well-known person, try to read up on him in advance of the interview. Take notes so that you know as much about his background and his views on various subjects as possible. Also, take note of the questions other interviewers have asked in the past.

Then make sure that when you finally meet the interviewee, you don't ask the same old things. And start your talk by mentioning a few of the things you learned in your research. This will be flattering to the interviewee and is almost certainly guaranteed to start things off on the right track.

Look for a fresh angle of discussion. But if you start off in one direction and your interviewee proceeds in another, let him go for a while. Who knows? He may reveal a side of himself which has never before come to light. This is where top interviewers separate themselves from the crowd—their instinctive ability to get their subject talking.

Some writers will tell you that using a tape recorder will get the subject "up tight." In some cases, this is true, especially if you use one of the older recorders which require a microphone at the end of a cord. The mike sits in front of the subject, constantly reminding him that he is being recorded.

Invest a few dollars and get yourself one of the new compact recorders with built-in resistor mikes. These recorders are often no larger than a pocket camera, completely quiet and inconspicuous, and yet they will record up to an hour without flipping the tape.

We should point out that federal law requires you to advise people when you are recording them, so mention it in an offhand way when you first start talking. Within minutes your subject will forget all about it.

Equally distracting for some interviewees is the writer who copiously takes notes throughout the conversation. We've seen some writers who actually halt their subject in mid-sentence while they catch up on their writing. Fortunately, most experienced reporters have developed their own form of shorthand so that they can keep up with all but the fastest talkers. But even so, note-taking can be distracting. And it is a constant reminder to the interviewee that everything he says may appear in print.

For this reason, some writers prefer to use neither notes nor recorder, but prefer to record the conversation mentally. Following the interview, they get to a typewriter and type everything down while it is still fresh in their mind. This technique can create serious problems, even if you have an impeccable memory. Should the subject claim later that he was misquoted, you have no proof that what you wrote is what he said. And, if your memory is less than perfect, you could wind up with a libel suit on your hands, if your subject cares to pursue matters.

To protect yourself, the safest method is to record the interview. And do not agree to surrender the tape or to present a rough draft of your column or article for approval prior to publication. To do so is to invite all kinds of problems—your subject may demand that something he said on the record later be taken off or he may want to edit or completely rewrite your material. (It's amazing how many basketball players and politicians suddenly get the urge to write after they see how you've done it.)

Finally, mark and file each recorded interview. Tapes cost just a dollar or two, but they can save you a lot of grief if they are available should a problem develop. Some writers reuse their tapes as soon as the story appears, but that can be dangerous, since in most states, suit can be filed up to two years following publication of an article which is felt to be libelous or slanderous.

Here are a few other hints for conducting a successful interview:

• Don't interrupt your subject. If he starts "rapping," let him go.
• Don't get entangled in an argument. If your subject says something that offends you, learn to ignore it. You are there to interview him, not debate him.
• Dress appropriately for the occasion. If you are interviewing a businessman, don't show up in jeans and a sweater. If you are interviewing a gas station attendant, wear jeans and a sweater rather than a business suit. In short, make your subject feel comfortable with you.
•Keep your questions simple and easily understood. Don't pull a William Buckley on your subject.

What about telephone interviews? If you can't get the interview any other way, then the telephone is better than nothing. But face-to-face interaction produces the best results in almost all cases. The only exceptions are when you are interviewing someone who is a fanatical cause promoter or a pathological liar.

You won't be able to see the expression on your subject's face when you ask a sensitive question over the phone. Nor will you be able to size him up by his "body language" as the interview progresses. And many top writers actually use a lot of the peripheral goings-on in building the color of their article or column.

5

A special breed

In the newspaper game, there are reporters, and then there are Reporters with a capital R. Reporters with a capital R are generally the ones who eventually wind up writing columns. They usually don't become editorial writers because that discipline is much too restricting for their talents as a storyteller and painter with words.

A top reporter will become a top columnist. Why? Because it takes the same basic skills, the same instincts, the same determination to write a page one news story as it does to write a memorable column, regardless of whether that column deals with corruption in government or growing a prize-winning rose.

The star columnist, like the star reporter, has a "nose for news," as the old-timers on the copy desk like to say. He always seems to be at the right place and at the right time. Sometimes, it is planned that way. Other times, it seems to be mere coincidence.

But it is more than that. The real newsman is enthusiastic

about his job—so much so that he doesn't think about what time it is or how much time he has put in that day or week. If he hears a siren on his way home, he'll follow it just to see what's going on. He has a camera in his glove compartment that is loaded with fast film—just in case. He also has a tape recorder and note pad with him. If he stumbles onto something, he sticks with it.

Top reporters and columnists have other attributes:

• They know how to spell.

• They work on more than one story or column idea at a time. They have many in the planning stages, and they put the pieces together for each according to its own timetable.

• They have a large list of sources that they are able to call on whenever necessary. And their sources know that if something is told in confidence, the newsman will not divulge his source, regardless of consequences. (Many a journalist has gone to jail for contempt of court rather than divulge his sources at the order of a judge.) And, unless you are an investigative reporter or muckraking columnist such as Jack Anderson, you should not let yourself be tricked into receiving information "off the record." That is just a ploy of sharp operators who pretend they are doing you a favor by telling you something off the record, when in fact they are really protecting themselves by getting your assurance that you won't divulge the information. Usually, it is something you could have obtained from another source who would have been "on the record." Best way to avoid this trap is to simply stop someone who says he will tell you something off the record and advise him that unless it is on the record, to keep it to himself, and you will get it somewhere else. They will almost always "come across."

• When you stumble across an idea for a column, *write it down*. Otherwise, you may forget all about it in the rush to get another story.

•People are always more interesting than inanimate objects. So try to build your column around a person rather than an object.

•Remember that there is no one single "right" way to write a column or a story. If you complete a column and it just doesn't hang together right, rewrite it from a different angle.

• Everyone makes mistakes, even top columnists. You may recall not too long ago that Washington columnist Jack Anderson blew the whistle on a well-known politician, only to learn later that his source had fed him hearsay information. Anderson bit the bullet and apologized publicly—in print as well as on TV. If you goof, admit it and apologize if that is called for.

• Another essential ingredient of a top columnist is the willingness to dig, dig, dig for information, and then the extra effort required to verify what he uncovers.

A great example of dogged determination to get a story is the true account of Michael Mok of the *New York Daily News.* He was assigned to interview an obese individual who was trying to lose weight by isolating himself aboard a sloop in Long Island Sound. Mok's outboard-powered rowboat conked out about a mile from the sloop and the deadline was fast approaching. So Mok dived into the 40-degree water and swam the remaining distance, almost drowning in the process. But he got his story *and* made his deadline. Now that's what is meant by dogged determination! It explains why war correspondents such as the late Ernie Pyle and cartoonist Bill Mauldin outshone their competitors. They went out to the troops at the front instead of staying safely back at headquarters and accepting handouts from the PIO officer.

In looking back on our own experiences, we realize that our best stories were the ones we had to work hardest for. We used to cover the police beat by riding with one of the cops in a patrol car. Once it paid off with a first-hand account of a gunman who held a family hostage all day before he was gunned down himself. Then there was the time we arrived at the scene of a burglary with the police and helped to capture three armed robbers. Another time, the two of us had a chance for an exclusive interview with ski racer Jean-Claude Killy *if* we could be in Breckenridge, Colo., the next morning. We were broke, so we drove nonstop from Chicago (a distance of some 1,200 miles). We had to chase Killy all the way to Steamboat Springs but we got our story! There were plenty of other experiences, too. Like the time one of us went all the way into the remote reaches of the Bugaboo Mountains of British Columbia to get a story on wilderness skiing. We almost got buried in an avalanche, and a timber wolf stalked us (coming within 20 feet), but again, we came back with one helluva story!

In writing, just as in any other endeavor, it is usually the people who put out the greatest effort who reap the greatest rewards.

Going under cover

Eventually, almost every serious journalist, be he reporter or feature writer or columnist, decides that to get a particular story, he must go under cover. The best recent example of this kind of reporting is the infamous Mirage bar caper, carried out by a team of *Chicago Sun-Times* investigative reporters and photographers. The paper actually put up the money to purchase the tavern, and then had its people go under cover to operate it. In the months that followed, the team uncovered rampant payoffs, bribes, and other "requirements" of doing business in Chicago. As a result of the major series of articles that followed, a sweeping shakeup of all levels of city government took place and corruption was ended—at least for a while.

Another classic case, which also took place in Chicago, involved a reporter taking a job as an attendant in a nursing home. His investigation revealed shocking treatment of patients and resulted in another sweeping shakeup in nursing home operations.

Reporters and columnists have been known to infiltrate subversive organizations, to literally go to jail to uncover corruption in the prison system. Hunter Thompson of the *Village Voice* rode with the infamous Hell's Angels outlaw motorcycle gang for 18 months to gather information for a series of articles and a later book.

Generally, going under cover should never be undertaken by an individual without assistance from other journalists, and also preferably with the blessing and support of a newspaper (or in this case a syndicate). Even then, such a move can be risky, to say the least. And even after the lengthy probe, you could still come away with no story or a story of minor consequence.

6

Putting it all together

So far, we've discussed the techniques of writing a column and the things to keep in mind in gathering information for a column. But it takes more than a group of individual columns to make a syndicated columnist. There must be some sort of glue, something that gives your work a sense of continuity over the long haul. Granted, you are writing about a particular subject area, but that still leaves you with a lot of ground to cover. Your aim should be to develop a cadre of loyal readers who follow your column faithfully from day to day or week to week.

The trick is to plan ahead, perhaps as far as a year or more, so that there is continuity in the direction of your individual columns. They should fit together like the pieces of a puzzle, similar in many respects to a series of feature articles devoted to a particular subject.

At the same time, each column should be able to stand on its own merits and as a separate entity, so that the occasional reader or the brand new reader can "jump in" without difficulty. In some respects you could liken the continuing syndicated column to one of the daytime TV soap operas. They are written so that each episode leads you into the next, but so that if you miss two weeks of your favorite show, you can take up again without really missing all that much.

Develop a distinct style

Part of giving your column its own personality is developing your own special style of writing it. The style should be such that you are not restricted to any one particular format, such as the interview or the narrative re-creation, but have the freedom to take any approach you want, still enabling your readers to recognize your writing even if they can't see your by-line. A distinct style helps the reader to identify with the column. Like a well-worn pair of shoes, it feels comfortable. He knows what to expect.

How often?

The decision of how often your column should run will depend on a wide variety of factors. How timely is the content? How difficult is each column to research and write? Most important, how does your syndicate (or its participating newspapers) feel about frequency of publication?

If your subject matter is seasonal in nature, such as snow skiing or gardening, when should the column begin and when should it end for the season? In the case of skiing, for example, it may seem odd, but most columns start in mid-October—in time for the annual ski shows which take place across the country—and they usually wrap up in mid-March, when most Midwest and eastern ski resorts are closing down and the Western mountain resorts are into their final few weeks of operation. Seasonal column dates will depend on many factors, but chief among them is how advertisers feel. If garden suppliers, for example, want to start running their ads in late February, that's when the editors will want to start related editorial material.

Don't count on your syndicate editor to advise you on this. You should do your own research and then present it along with your proposal and sample columns.

Generally, daily columns are limited to political columns, with the exception of such "hot" items as Ann Landers, Dr. Joyce Brothers, and other popular psychology and advice columns. Other columns which lend themselves to daily publication would be those dealing with astrology, "This Date in History," and so on.

Weekly columns encompass most other topics, with the exception of limited interest columns, such as those devoted to things like model railroading, stamp collecting, and the like. Part of your job in planning ahead is to make sure you don't miss any bets in tying columns in with important dates and holidays of all types. You should also take into account the various seasonal changes and any other time factors which will affect the direction of your subject matter.

You should maintain a log of upcoming columns and try to stay well ahead of the deadlines set for you by your syndicate editor. If you are selling your column directly, then you will have the sole responsibility to make sure the columns go out on time. As insurance, you really should prepare a half dozen or so timeless columns which can be used by participating newspapers in an emergency, such as a postal strike or natural disaster which delays delivery of the mails. These should be submitted and then sent out by the syndicate. You should also have another dozen or so "in reserve," in case you become ill or are injured.

In the case of a lengthy illness or serious injury, it will be up to your syndicate to get a replacement to fill in. Make sure you protect yourself in case of such an eventuality by requiring that the contract you sign specifies that you are the sole owner of the column and its title, and that in event of injury or illness, you are to retain ownership even though a substitute writer takes your place temporarily.

Visual aids

Included as visual aids are photos, cartoons, charts, graphs, and various other types of illustrations. Generally, it is the responsibility of the syndicated columnist to provide such materials. Some columns don't need visual aids, while others (business, travel, and science columns) are obviously better with them.

In negotiating with a syndicate, you should discuss the need for various visual aids. If the syndicate requests them, you can do one of two things: hire photographers and illustrators on your own and figure their cost into your own requirement for payment; or ask the syndicate to hire a person or persons directly to work with their editor to produce materials for your various columns. Here again, the need for advance planning and a long-range list of column topics is essential so that illustrators and photographers have time to produce collateral materials.

7

Freebies and other "fringe benefits"

Every journalist is faced with the problem of dealing with various kinds of gratuities and gifts. To take or not to take; that is the question. But the answer is not a simple yes or no.

For one thing, the kind of things that fall into the general category of freebies ranges from press passes and complimentary tickets to events, to all-expenses-paid junkets to destinations near and far. It is common practice, especially in large cities, for police departments to issue large PRESS cards to be placed on the dashboards of cars belonging to reporters and photographers. Such cards usually, but not always, result in the car not being ticketed or towed when parked in an illegal area. Many syndicated columnists, especially those in Washington, D.C., often get such dashboard cards.

There are also wallet-sized press cards issued by the major wire services, some syndicates, and virtually all newspapers for their editorial staffers. Flashing such cards often gets one past ushers and guards at such events as football games, trade shows, circuses, and even private parties and banquets. When a journalist shows up to cover an event, he is usually given preferred treatment, ranging from not waiting in line for entrance, to getting a free meal in the case of banquets.

Generally speaking, the more important an individual journalist is to a corporation, a lobbying group, a politician, or any other individual or organization, the more that journalist will be courted. And since the kingpins of journalism are the syndicated political columnists, they are most likely to be offered anything from a free junket to an outright bribe. (Much as we'd like to say that all journalists are noble idealists, the truth is that we're really just like everyone else. A certain percentage of journalists is on the take.)

The question to be faced by you as an individual syndicated columnist or feature writer is simply where to draw the line. Some newsmen and organizations say flatly that they will accept nothing, period. Frankly, we think that attitude is a bit extreme. If you are legitimately covering an event, why shouldn't you have free access? On the other hand, if you are going to a baseball game or a horse race strictly as a fan, we think you should pay your way like everyone else.

Gifts may be accepted at Christmas and other special occasions from those close enough that you give gifts of equal value in return. But, if you write a weekly column on agriculture, and a manufacturer of farm machinery sends your wife a mink stole for Christmas, don't think twice—return it!

Junkets, or trips of various lengths and duration, are another matter. What if you are an automotive writer, and American Motors Corp. invites you to an all-expenses-paid junket to get a look at their new models? Should you go? Well, AMC did just that a year or two ago, and most of the top automotive writers and columnists did accept their invitation, many adding the stipulation that they would be under no obligation regarding what they wrote about the new cars. Others went, but insisted on paying their own way. We tend to agree with the rationale of those who accepted AMC's offer that it was stressed that there were no special favors expected of the writers and that the sole purpose of the offer was to enable as many writers as possible to take a close look at the cars and then report their findings to their readers.

It is true that without the "subsidy," many of the writers would not have been able to afford the trip. And it is also true that their readers welcomed the opportunity to learn more about the new cars. But, on the other side of the coin, even though no favors were sought, there is no way that those who were treated so well would not be influenced in their viewpoints, at least a little. So here is an example of one of those gray areas, where each journalist must evaluate matters with his own conscience. Is it really so much different from Congressmen who visit foreign countries and are then given the red carpet treatment and sometimes loaded down with gifts of all types?

What about the matter of smaller freebies, such as a free lunch? Generally, a good rule to follow is if you are invited to discuss something over lunch with a news source, it is okay if he picks up the tab. On the other hand, if you request the luncheon meeting, for whatever reason, you should pay for both of you. (And after all, it *is* tax deductible.)

This also brings up the matter of record keeping for tax purposes. Regardless of whether you syndicate your column, or sell it on your own to individual papers, or you do other types of freelance work, you should keep detailed records of all business-related expenses, including all travel and entertainment.

Dealing with the IRS

If you are like most creative people, you probably regard the matter of keeping ledgers and other records as a nuisance at best, and more likely a confusing, frustrating chore. Because of this distaste for record keeping, most writers, actors, photographers, painters and other creative types do a poor to rotten job of keeping their financial affairs in order.

The net result is that you not only suffer monthly mental strain, but your pocketbook gets short-changed in the long run. Every single deductible expense you forget to record, every receipt you don't bother to ask for, costs you hard cash when your accountant sits down to prepare your state and federal tax returns. And the higher your income bracket, the more each omission costs you.

The classic example of the disorganized, lackadaisical writer is the Neil Simon character Oscar Madison of "The Odd Couple." In one of the TV episodes, Oscar is audited and must bring his records down to the IRS office. He dumps desk drawers, wastebaskets and shoe boxes into a large cardboard container and presents this mess to the agent. You can imagine the reaction!

Believe it or not, a lot of our own writer friends are almost this bad in real life. Obviously if they do get called in to explain their tax deductions, they are in one hell of a fix.

Record keeping need not be as bad as you might believe. For starters, set aside 10 minutes at the end of each working day. Take all the various receipts you have collected and log them in one of three separate journals—one for travel, a second for entertainment and a third for other expenses. The books need not be elaborate—simple spiral notebooks will do. Just make sure each entry includes the date, the amount spent, and the purpose for the expenditure. The best way to log each individual entry is with the date on the left side of the page, the explanation in the middle, and the dollar amount on the right.

Whenever possible, get a receipt as a backup record for the expense and keep the receipts in separate envelopes according to the month. If you have a great deal of receipts, break them down further according to category—travel, entertainment, or "other." Keep all the envelopes in a file drawer or cardboard container. You won't need them unless you are called in for a tax audit. Otherwise, your accountant can simply use your record books for figuring your return.

Actually, the only receipts the IRS requires you to keep are for expenses of $25 or more, but they will be much more inclined to accept your explanations of expenses if they see you have saved receipts for even small expenses. But it is important to remember that receipt or not, you *must* have a detailed record of even the smallest expenses, including tips, to get credit for them.

Travel

What kind of travel expenses are deductible for you as a columnist? The law says that *any* expense connected with a business trip can be deducted, even if the story doesn't pan out.

For example, air fare to and from an assignment or potential story can be written off, even if you fly first class. If you drive, you can deduct auto expenses in one of two ways—either by taking a "per mile" cost (check with IRS for current allowable amount) or by deducting a percentage of your total auto expenses per year, based on your evaluation of the percentage of driving which is business-related. Your accountant will also depreciate the value of your car over several years to give you an additional write-off.

Taking a percentage of your total auto expenses—including gas, oil, tune-ups, repairs, toll fees, parking fees, etc.—usually is the best way, since it eliminates the need for marking down starting mileage and finishing mileage for every business-related trip.

Hotel bills are also deductible, regardless of which hotel you stay in and how expensive the room, that is unless the IRS feels that you are being overly extravagant. But such cases are seldom argued. You will get an argument if you deduct the total cost of rooms and meals for you *and* a traveling companion, unless, of course, that person is needed on a professional basis.

Meals are also deductible, but here again, the IRS can call you if it feels you are being extravagant. (For example, if you have a habit of ordering $50 French champagne with your meals, you will catch some flak from the auditor.)

Tips of all kinds are also deductible, and here you can generally take up to 20 percent of the bill without question.

It may surprise you to learn that various other expenses while on the road can be deducted, including your own entertainment.

Let's say you take in a movie, or have a few drinks in the hotel bar before turning in. They are deductible, as long as you are away from home overnight. So are such other expenses as hair cuts, shaves, massages, steam room fees, and the like.

Entertainment

As you may have heard, the "three-martini lunch" has come under fire. But that doesn't mean you can't deduct the cost of entertaining news sources. Even the IRS accepts the fact that in order to get in good with some sources, they must be "wined and dined" occasionally to loosen their tongues. After all, without your sources you might be out of business, and then Uncle Sam would be paying you unemployment insurance instead of collecting tax money from you.

You need not necessarily get a great story every time you entertain a source, but your record book should at least indicate what you talked about and the potential story which could result.

Generally, you can deduct such things as dinner, drinks, and a night club show as well as tennis court fees, green fees, and other such entertainment costs.

And, crazy as it sounds, you can deduct payments to informants (other than public officials) whose information is needed for a story.

If you are fortunate enough to own a yacht, or a chalet in Aspen, you may only deduct the cost of entertaining plus the percentage of total maintenance attributable to entertaining, provided at least 51 percent of its total usage is for business purposes.

Other expenses

If you shoot your own photographs for your column, you can deduct the initial cost of all camera equipment, all repair bills, and all processing costs. And camera equipment may also be depreciated. Finally, camera equipment and other such gear (including typewriters) qualifies for the investment tax credit of 10 percent off the purchase price, over and above using the price as a standard deduction. The credit comes off your tax bill, not your gross income.

(You may recall that when President Jimmy Carter was running for office, his peanut business had so many investment tax credits from equipment purchases that Jimmy declared an income that year of $60,000, but didn't have to pay a *cent* in taxes. To show what a decent citizen he was, he volunteered to pay $6,000 to the IRS, even though he didn't have to.)

As a writer, you obviously must keep up with current events as well as developments in your particular subject area. If you subscribe to various magazines or professional journals, the cost is deductible. If you buy binoculars to cover an event, the cost is deductible.

If you are a golf writer who reviews golf courses, the cost of clubs, bag, cart, balls, even certain golf clothes is deductible, because you need them to do your job. The same is true of ski equipment for the ski or travel writer, fishing gear for the outdoor columnist, and so on. Of course, such writers usually get such equipment for free or at the "pro" rate anyway, but the deduction for any such costs still saves you money.

Any expenses connected with researching your subject are also deductible, including the cost of books, tapes, films, plus fees for copies of legal documents.

For all expenses which do not fall under easily recognizable categories, the rule is that if you must make the expense in the pursuit of your work, it is deductible. But when in doubt, always check with your accountant.

Working at home

Most free-lance writers and syndicated columnists maintain an office in their home, even if they also have an office elsewhere. The IRS is cracking down on what it will allow for deductions of home office space for self-employed individuals. Unless you can show that you really do use the office exclusively for business and not also for a den, you cannot deduct it.

If you turn a bedroom into an office, or you make an office in your attic or basement, you can deduct that percentage of the total space in the house that is used exclusively as an office. That means if 10 percent of your home is used for an office, you can deduct 10 percent of your mortgage fee or rent, 10 percent of your utilities bills (light and heat), plus whatever percentage of your phone bill is for business. (Be sure to save all detailed listings of long-distance calls and be prepared to tell to whom the call was made and for what purpose.)

If you build a darkroom in your home, the cost of construction plus the percentage of space it takes is deductible. If your garage is filled with paraphernalia connected with your writing, that space is deductible.

Miscellaneous

While there is no law against filing your own tax returns, we strongly suggest you use the services of a certified public accountant, preferably one with expertise in dealing with writers. He will be in a position to save you money because a) he will fill out your form correctly, and b) he is familiar with the latest changes in the tax laws. Best of all, if you do get called in for an audit, you can sign over the power of attorney to your accountant and let him do battle with the IRS people.

There is a good deal of wisdom in letting your accountant represent you in an audit. For one thing, he has prepared the return, so he is in the best position to explain any problem areas. And if the agent should ask him a tricky question, he can always defer by saying he'll have to check with you. That will give him and you time to come up with a satisfactory reply.

Our own accountant advises us to take advantage of every single deduction and loophole in filing our return. But he advises strongly against not declaring some of your income (such as the occasional free-lance article you may write). Chances are you'll never be caught, but occasionally the IRS does audit publishers and they have a nasty habit of checking a percentage of the free-lancers to make sure they are declaring their story fees.

If the IRS disallows a deduction, it just costs you money. If the IRS catches you not declaring income, you could go to jail!

8

Avoiding legal hassles

One inherent danger of writing a syndicated column is that, by its very nature, it gets wide exposure. That means you have to be doubly careful about every fact, every quote, every inference you make. Your column need not be of a controversial nature to get you into hot water and a possible lawsuit.

All syndicates carry liability insurance as do most publishers and many columnists. But the potential cost of a lawsuit is more than just dollars and cents. It is time (sometimes years) and aggravation, and who needs that? It is much wiser to do a little more homework, a little closer checking of facts, and a second or third rewrite to make sure you aren't violating the rights of an individual or an organization.

Libel

The most common legal action brought against writers and publishers is that of libel. Webster defines libel as any statement or representation published without just cause or excuse, or any pictures, effigies, or other signs tending to expose another to public hatred, contempt, or ridicule.

Please take particular note that it does not say anything about untrue statements. A lot of journalists labor under the mistaken notion that for a story to be libelous, it must contain untruths about a person. You can libel a person simply by stating the truth about him, if the result causes him to be held in public contempt, ridicule, or hatred—in short, damages his reputation.

The only people who must prove that the information published about them was false and defamatory are so-called "public persons," and "public figures." These include people in the hierarchy of government, or at least those in government with substantial control over governmental affairs; and persons who have achieved notoriety for their achievements or who have vigorously and successfully sought the public's attention.

The key to winning a libel suit in the case of public persons is the ability to prove "actual malice"—the publication of false defamatory material with knowledge that it was false or with reckless disregard of whether it was false or not.

In further expanding on this definition by the Supreme Court, the judges decreed that there must be proof that the information was published with a high degree of awareness of probable falsity; there must be sufficient evidence that the defendant had serious doubts as to the truth of his publication.

Invasion of privacy

With the nation's growing concerns over threats to our privacy, journalists must be ever more careful that what they report does not infringe on others' rights.

Based on previous court tests of privacy laws, an individual is protected as follows:

1. From appropriation of his name or likeness for advertising purposes or purposes of trade.

2. From intrusion, where the journalist "butts in" where he could not reasonably be expected.

3. From public revelation of private facts which are embarrassing, regardless of their truthfulness.

4. From being put in a false light in the public eye.

If you find yourself in a situation where you are unsure about yourself in a possible invasion of privacy, you have two options:

1. Ask your syndicate editor to check with his attorney for a clarification before you proceed.

2. Either rephrase your information or delete it from your column.

Some newsmen, especially old-timers, would shudder at such suggestions. The classic scenario would depict a cigar-chomping city editor reading the copy, nodding approval, then splashing the hot story across the top of page one.

Fortunately, newspapering has come a long way since the days of yellow journalism. Today's reporters and editors have a good deal more responsibility than their forebears. And the rule of thumb has become, "When in doubt, don't print it."

The other side to this coin is what some legal experts see as a threat to freedom of the press. For example, Dr. Arthur Miller of the Harvard Law School recently cited the following as cases of unwarranted uses of privacy restrictions:

1. Reverse freedom of information suits, as in the case of a hospital going to court to prevent a reporter from obtaining Medicare reports for informing the public about hospital costs.

2. The prevention of personal finance disclosure by political candidates and office holders.

3. Bans on the use of tape recorders by reporters.

What we have here is a case of the rights of individuals and the right of freedom of the press (designed to protect those same individuals) clashing. The only workable answer is restraint by all sides, even when it hurts a little.

Copyright laws

As a writer of a syndicated column, you definitely must protect your work so that it isn't "pirated" by publications which have not paid for it. Generally, the syndicate will file for copyright for you or itself, depending on the terms of your contract. Some writers retain rights to their work, while others sell all rights to the syndicate.

If your arrangement calls for you to handle copyright application, or if you are functioning as your own syndicate, here's what you have to know about copyrights:

A copyright is valid for the life of the author, plus an additional 50 years. So if you do produce some deathless prose, your heirs will be able to reap the rewards.

How do you copyright a column? Simply include the required copyright notice (the symbol ©, the word "Copyright" or the abbreviation "Copr.") as well as the year of publication and name of the copyright proprietor (your by-line) on all copies.

Technically, you are required to "promptly file" a claim to copyright along with a fee of $6 and two copies of the work for copyright protection. But there isn't any time limit. In one case, a publisher filed for a copyright 27 years after the original date the article was published and the court ruled it was still a "prompt filing."

It should be pointed out that if you do not file for copyright at the time of publication, you could be subject to a fine from the Register of Copyrights when you do file, and you won't be able to start litigation for copyright infringement until after you file. But thanks to the recently passed revision in copyright laws, the author is essentially protected from the time he writes a piece.

Part 2

Selling
your column

The first part of this book dealt with the creation of your column, from selection of subject matter to its development. Part 2 tells you how to successfully sell your creation.

9

The nature of the beast

The title of this chapter refers to the syndicates, not the column or the columnist. After all, as Caesar or some other famous general once said, "Know thine enemy." Or, putting it another way, if you really expect to sell your idea to a syndicate, you should know something about how syndicates operate beforehand.

Their structure

Syndicates, like news services, are a good deal like the newspapers they serve, at least insomuch as they have parallel chains of command, an editorial and a sales staff. And just as newspapers can be daily or weekly, syndicates come in two basic types—the corporation-owned and the independent variety.

Syndicates such as the Chicago Tribune Syndicate and King Features are part of a major organization which includes a chain of newspapers. Independent syndicates, like independent papers, are usually smaller by comparison, but in most other respects are very much like their big brothers.

Columnists and feature writers have deadlines to meet (usually one to five weeks in advance of its release in subscribing newspapers), just like their counterparts on those newspapers. And copy editors must process this steady flow of incoming copy, photos, and illustrations.

Correspondence from would-be columnists and feature writers is funneled to a special department, where it is screened. The hot prospects find their way to the top editor's office, while the remainder are returned, sometimes with a detailed explanation why it was rejected, and sometimes with just a form letter.

Whenever you submit an idea for a syndicated column or feature, always include a stamped, addressed envelope if you want your materials returned. It really isn't fair to expect the syndicate to foot the bill for sending back scores of packets each week, partly because of the expense and partly because of the time required.

An important department of the syndicate is that which deals with promoting new features and columns. Once a column is accepted, up to a dozen samples are set in type and sent with a promotional folder or brochure to hundreds of potential buyers across the country. Meanwhile, the syndicates' sales reps get on the phone, and occasionally make personal calls, in an effort to sign up as many participating papers as possible.

Editors are people, too

The cliche portrayal of editors of all genre tends to be like that played by the late Clark Gable in the movie *Teacher's Pet,* or more recently by Ed Asner in the TV series "Lou Grant." You know the type—surly, opinionated, hard-nosed, slightly disheveled, but a terrific newsman.

There really are editors who fit this mold, but they are in the minority. Between the two of us, we've worked for a dozen or more editors and know many more. Their personalities and quirks are as varied as in any other group of people. If there are certain characteristics which are more or less common to all of them, they would be a basic enjoyment of their work and a proclivity for procrastinating when it comes to nonessential chores.

Most editors with syndicates cut their eye teeth on the copy desks of newspapers and then opt for the syndicate because of better hours, less pressure, and generally better pay. One thing they bring with them is the ability to recognize good writing.

Don't assume that your material will not get a fair shake. It may not be read in total, but an experienced editor doesn't have to read it all to know whether or not it has merit. If he likes it, then it will be passed on to a higher editor where it will very definitely get a thorough going-over before a decision is made one way or the other.

And don't assume that because you aren't an established name in the business (a Jimmy Breslin or a Rex Reed) that your material will be given short shrift. Syndicates need new stars, and they have to find a certain number each year in order to compete successfully with the hundreds of other syndicates and news services that serve the country's newspapers.

Rates

Rates fall into two categories—those paid by the newspapers to the syndicates for use of material, and those paid by the syndicates to their writers.

The syndicate bases its price to the newspaper on the paper's circulation. The cost can run from as little as five cents per thousand readers on up, with no limit other than the willingness of the publisher to pay for whatever is offered. The advantage of this form of sliding scale is that it enables the small town paper to have access to important columnists and feature writers just as the major big city papers do.

The big papers don't complain about the pricing system because they realize that their own cost is considerably lower when the syndicate is able to sell the same material to many papers across the country.

One thing that almost all syndicates offer their customers is a certain territorial protection. For example, the same column would not be sold to competing papers in the same city, because then neither would have anything special for hooking new readers or keeping old ones. Territorial protection is even offered in the case where two papers are close enough that their circulation areas overlap. Before a syndicate will sell a column to both such papers, it will make sure that both agree beforehand.

Of course, not all columns start at the same cost per thousand (CPM) or end at the same level. The syndicate determines its cost according to the author and subject matter. If Reggie Jackson were to write a column on baseball, for example, it would command a higher CPM figure than one written by an unknown. And a column on chess will not command the same fee as one on finance or marriage.

The columnist can be paid in a variety of ways, from a flat fee, to a regular salary, to a commission (the most common). Fees can be calculated according to the number of words, or per column. Commissions are usually based on a percent of the net or gross revenue generated. (In the case of payment on net, the cost of typesetting, printing, and preparation of photo mats or PMTs is deducted before determining commission. Such other expenses as salaries of syndicate employees, office rent, promotional campaigns and the like are borne by the syndicate from its share of revenues generated by the sale of materials to papers.)

Commissions can range up and down the scale, but generally, a new columnist should not expect to be offered more than 40 percent of net, or 50 percent tops, in the case of an obviously hot column.

If your column idea turns out to be a good seller, you will see your monthly commission checks increasing as more papers take on the column. But if you really think you may have a potential blockbuster on your hands, you should negotiate for a short-term contract. That way, you can push for a greater percentage when the contract comes up for renewal.

You would also be wise to make sure your contract gives you ownership of the concept of the column as well as its title, so that if you ever do part company with your syndicate, you can take your column with you.

As for revenue generated by additional use of the column, such as in reprint, advertising, novelties, and the like, the custom is for syndicates to retain a percentage. After all, the success of your column is a combined effort of you as writer and the syndicate as sales vehicle. It is only fair that both share in whatever revenues are generated.

Other syndicated features

Syndicates are best known for the columns they sell to newspapers, but they sell other material as well. Chief among these is the feature article or feature series. Other material includes photos and illustrations.

With hundreds of syndicates buying material on a continuing basis, the need for fresh articles and photos is never-ending. In fact, your chances of selling individual features or feature series is a good deal better than selling a column idea. The chief advantage of producing a column is that is provides a certain guarantee of income and it eliminates the need to resell yourself every time you have a new idea.

If you aren't successful in selling your column ideas, you should consider selling for a while as a feature writer. Then, when you have established yourself with one or more syndicates, query them on column ideas. Your chances will be greatly improved.

10

Selling your ideas

You may have the greatest idea for a feature, series of features, or column, but unless you can convince the syndicate, your idea isn't worth a dime. To crack the world of the syndicate writer, you have to have three things going for you: good ideas, writing talent, and salesmanship. Eliminate any of the three and you will strike out. Put all three together and you have a 50-50 chance of hitting a home run.

Packaging the product

You've no doubt heard the story about Abe Lincoln writing the Gettysburg Address on a scrap of paper as he was riding in a train to the site of the battle. And movies have depicted the struggling author using old paper bags or anything else he can find to produce his epic.

In the real world of today, slick packaging is an essential sales tool, and that includes the writer, too. A lot of rules for getting a job apply to selling your column or feature ideas. For example:

Your only contact, at least at first, with the syndicate people will be by mail. Your letters and manuscripts are you, at least as far as they are concerned.

What would happen if you were to reply to an ad for a job on a newspaper or magazine editorial staff and you wrote in longhand? Or your letter was typed with a machine that had a worn-out ribbon and a few bent keys? And suppose the paper was wrinkled, and maybe had a smudge or a stain on it? Worst of all, suppose your correspondence contained several misspelled words? Not only would you not get the job, you wouldn't even get as far as the interview.

The same holds true for selling your ideas to a syndicate. Your correspondence should tell the reader that here is a really sharp individual.

Contents

There are several ways to go about presenting your ideas to a syndicate. One is by sending a query letter that briefly explains what you have in mind. The second way is to send a cover letter, along with several samples of your column, plus a stamped, addressed envelope for return of the materials. A third way is to call the syndicate editor and discuss your concept before sending anything.

Of the three, we favor the second—sending a complete packet. Some people will argue that an editor is less likely to wade through such a submission, but, as we mentioned earlier, he doesn't have to read it all to get an idea of whether he likes it or not. Then, if the packet gets sent higher up for further evaluation, everything is right there for them to see.

Type your sample columns on plain, white paper. Use a substantial weight, not onionskin or other flimsy paper. Double space for ease of reading and for possible corrections or comments by editors. Indicate "more" at the bottom of each individual page except the final page of each column. Use a hatch mark (#) or the designation -30- at the bottom of the final page of copy. Number your pages in the upper right-hand corner, or use the newspaper system ("add 1" for page 2, "add 2" for page 3, and so on).

Make a carbon or other copy of everything you submit, just in case it is either lost in the mail or is not returned for one reason or another.

Use a separate letterhead for your cover letter. Spend a few dollars and have your own stationery printed. It will make a much better impression than simply typing on plain paper.

Don't try to fold your packet so it will fit into a standard business envelope. Buy a 9 × 12 envelope and place everything flat with a piece of cardboard in front and back of your manuscripts, using rubber bands to hold it together. This way, your materials won't be "folded, bent, or mutilated" when they arrive and your neat packet of materials will make a favorable impression.

Writing a business letter is an art unto itself. Just remember that you are selling yourself as a professional writer. That implies that you know how to be brief. Your cover letter should be no longer than one page. If your concept for a column is detailed, why not present it as a separate proposal attached to the cover letter?

You might also want to include a proposed schedule of columns for several months, just so your reader (the syndicate editor) knows that you aren't just shooting in the dark with an idea and really can't produce a continuing string of columns.

Should you enclose a resume of your background? We think you should simply cite your credentials briefly in your cover letter. As we've said already, understatement works better than the hard sell. But have a resume ready, in case you are later asked to submit one.

Generally, all communications, including negotiations for payment, can be handled by mail. You may wish to meet personally as a final step before signing a contract, especially if you feel you want a lawyer to check the contract. But do not make the mistake of barging into the office of a particular syndicate in hopes of seeing someone who can listen to your idea or look over your materials. It is a sure way to blackball yourself. Follow accepted procedures and your chances of a sale will be greatly improved.

Can you trust them?

A lot of writers worry that by sending their carefully developed idea for a column to a total stranger, they are leaving themselves open to be ripped off. The chances of this sort of thing happening are almost nil.

For one thing, syndicates are not in the business of writing. They are in the business of selling what others write. They really don't want to be bothered with having to produce your idea. As for individual editors, their forte is correcting and improving others' work. They know how to write, but they are editors because either they enjoy editing more or they realize they are better at this end of the writing game. Besides, they know that if they try to pirate your idea, they are leaving themselves open to a lawsuit. (They do not know whether you have shown your work to others, or submitted it to other syndicates.)

It is possible that the syndicate will like your idea for a column, but not your style of writing. In such a situation, they may offer to buy your idea and then have another writer produce it. But you don't have to sell. If you say no, they will not proceed.

Waiting for an answer

Waiting to hear from a syndicate after you submit your idea and/or samples is like waiting for a refund check from the IRS. You know it's due, but there is no way of telling when it will arrive.

Most syndicates are deluged with correspondence of all types. Chances are you are more apt to hear from them quickly if they *don't* like your idea. If it has been three or four weeks and no word has come, it's a good bet that your material is getting a close going-over.

If six weeks go by with no word at all, you may call to inquire. It is possible the materials were lost in the mail, or mislaid somewhere in the office. In any case, the call will provide an answer one way or the other.

The shotgun approach

Should you limit your submission of the same idea and samples to one syndicate at a time? Some editors think so, but frankly, you may have to contact a dozen or more before you get a nibble. And if you deal with one at a time and it takes a total of two months each to get a final answer plus your materials back, you are talking about a two-year time lapse!

Many column ideas are timely, and in two years they may no longer be valid. We suggest you type up a half dozen duplicate samples and cover letters and send them out at the same time. As some come back, send them back out with a fresh cover letter to a different syndicate. You will be able to cover much more territory in a given period of time and at the same time increase your chance for a sale.

What if you hear from more than one syndicate who wants you to write for them? Simply advise each that you are definitely interested but that you have also been approached by another syndicate. You intend to discuss terms with both and then to make your decision based on the offer and the potential of each syndicate to produce sales to various papers.

In short, should such an eventuality occur, you will be in a much better bargaining position, newcomer or not.

11

Going it alone

Suppose that, within a reasonable period of time after contacting many syndicates with your idea, no one takes you up on your offer to write for them. Does that necessarily mean you must scrap your column?

There is another way to produce your column: Act as your own syndicate and sell it directly to newspapers instead of going through an intermediary. This is difficult and time-consuming, but it is not impossible. If you really have faith in your column, it can be done.

You might think that without the clout and prestige of a big-time syndicate to promote your column, you won't have a prayer of selling it to newspaper editors. Most editors couldn't care less whether your material comes from King Features Syndicate or from a little town in Nebraska, as long as a) it deals with a topic of special interest to their readers and b) it is well written.

The key to selling your column is to present it properly. And that means designing a sales package that shows off your wares and presents them in a manner that an editor can sort out and evaluate quickly. With several hundred syndicates, plus free-lance writers funneling material to newspapers on a regular basis, editors just do not have the time or the temperament to spend more than a few minutes on your package. So it must deliver its message *now!*

Perhaps the best way to get a visual idea of how good-looking sales kits look is to write to some of the better magazines and ask their ad department to send you a current media kit. These are created to sell media buyers at advertising agencies on the value of placing ads for various clients in a specific magazine. Such kits contain sample issues, rate cards, mechanical specs for ads, demographic information on readership, circulation break-downs, reader surveys and similar information.

To be successful, the media kit must contain all the information required to permit media planners to evaluate the magazine, and equally important, it must be presented properly.

By studying a number of media kits, you can get an idea of how your own sales packet ought to be designed to best sell editors. It should contain the following:

1. A half dozen sample columns, set in various type styles and widths (most commonly used by papers are 11 picas, 14 picas, and 20 picas wide), plus one or two typed samples.

Smaller publishers may want to simply paste up your typeset columns, while larger papers will usually want a typewritten version which can be edited by its own copy desk and then set in type in its own composing room so that it looks just like the "home grown" material.

2. Samples of photos, charts, graphs, and illustrations which are typical of those you anticipate being part of future columns.

3. A one-page resume of your background and experience. If you have a strong writing background, indicate it. If you aren't an established writer, but you do offer a special expertise in the subject matter of your column, concentrate on that aspect.

4. Include an 8 × 10 black-and-white glossy photo of yourself (head and shoulders only), especially if the photo helps sell you in relation to the column. (For example, a jockey in racing silks would be terrific to help promote a column on horse racing.)

Should the editor purchase your column, he may decide to use the photo regularly in a column head or occasionally to provide reader identification with you.

5. A cover letter or announcement which summarizes the content of your column and tells the editor the reasons his readers will want to read it. Be positive, let your enthusiasm show, but don't fill the letter or announcement with what editors call "puff." If you fall back on such words as "fabulous, far-reaching, unique" and other hackneyed vocabulary, the editor is almost sure to toss your material right into the wastebasket. He already has enough young reporters he's trying to teach how to write and doesn't need the same from a columnist.

6. A contract and order form, plus stamped, addressed envelope so that the editor can buy your column without resorting to typing his own envelope and writing a letter in return. Very few editors, even on the larger newspapers, have their own secretaries. Almost all handle their own correspondence, and, as a result, look for every way of avoiding such chores. Your order form and return envelope will help.

7. A 9 × 12 folder, preferably with pockets, that contains all of the other ingredients of your sales packet, arranged so that the editor can peruse it without rifling back and forth through a sheaf of paper. Put all the samples on one side and the other materials on the other side. The cover letter/announcement should be on top, followed by your resume and photo, and then the contract, order form, and return envelope.

The entire packet should be mailed in a 10 × 13 envelope, with the return address typed clearly in the upper left-hand corner. Type—do not write or print—the editor's name and address.

You may simply use your own name for the return address, or you may elect to give your new enterprise a more "official-sounding" name, such as J. B. Features or J. B., Inc. The theory here is that the materials are more apt to be given serious consideration if it appears that they come from an established organization rather than a struggling individual.

Frankly, we don't buy this line of reasoning expressed by some columnists. A check of a dozen newspaper editors in the Chicago area convinced us that as long as the packet is presented in a professional manner, it will be read and evaluated.

Other sales methods

Sending your sales packets directly to editors of newspapers is a form of direct-mail marketing. It will get results, but it is costly. If you figure that the cost of each individual packet is between $2 and $5, the cost of mailing is $1 or so, and you send 1,000 packets out, you can see how your own cost could run to $4,000 or $5,000.

And, if you accept the old marketing axiom that a 3% return on direct mail pieces is pretty good, you can see that such an approach might logically be expected to result in 30 sales. That's not really too bad, but it will take you a long, long time to recoup your investment. So, what other methods should you consider in selling your column?

Advertising pays

If it didn't, America's largest corporations wouldn't spend billions to deliver their sales messages via all forms of media. You can sell your column by advertising in trade journals which are read by newspaper and magazine editors. A number of such publications exist, but, by far, the most widely read is *Editor & Publisher,* a weekly magazine which reaches thousands of editors at papers large and small.

E&P has a special section of its classified ad columns entitled "Features Available." This section offers columns, puzzles, and other special features for sale. And they are often offered by individuals rather than by syndicates.

Here are a few examples:

Mind matter—Interesting questions-answers on personal relations by eminent psychologist. Helpful answers to vexing problems; gentle humor. Exceptional weekly column. 350 words. Send for FREE samples, low rates. F&N, 1640 Statler-Hilton, Buffalo, N. Y. 14202.

Real estate—For a consumer-oriented column that isn't antibusiness, write I. H. Paige, 7022 Ridge Blvd., Brooklyn, N. Y. 11209. Free samples, low rates.

Weekly—You can Do It, weekly handyman column. Inexpensive. Sample. Whitford, Box 745, Salem, Mass. 01970.

E&P charges between $2.10 and $2.60 per line, depending on number of lines and number of insertions, but you can see that the cost of running such advertising is certainly a fraction of the direct-mail approach.

Knocking on doors

This approach is the oldest sales approach known to man, but it still produces the best results. There is nothing like a face-to-face presentation of your ideas to an editor to sell your column. Your knowledge of the subject matter and your enthusiasm are best presented in this way. The editor will be flattered that you took the time to talk to him personally and that will work in your favor.

But don't just barge in on him. Call ahead for an appointment. Explain that you want to present a column idea with samples and that you would like 10 or 15 minutes of his time. Nine times out of ten, you'll get your appointment. And by calling ahead, you won't be interrupting him right at deadline time or when he's rushing to make an important meeting.

Don't invite him to lunch, or you'll go broke in short order. Editors have voracious appetites, equaled only by their thirst. Besides, editors don't expect to be wined and dined, and some may even take offense, assuming you are trying to buy their favor.

Knocking on doors has its problems. For one thing, you will soon run out of newspapers close to home and will eventually be required to go on the road. In order to make a road trip pay, you should plan an itinerary that gets you in to see as many editors per day as possible. And don't exclude evening calls: editors of A.M. papers usually work from 4 P.M. to midnight or so and that's when they are available.

Keep a detailed travel log, including all expenses. It's all deductible, and when your column starts returning a good income, you'll want every possible write-off.

The shotgun approach

The best, or at least the safest way to go about your selling task is to hedge your bets, the way investors do on the stock market. Don't put all your energy and money into a single sales approach, but instead use the "shotgun method." This means you should send out as many direct mail pieces, knock on as many doors, and run as many ads in trade journals as your budget and time will allow.

How much to charge

The determination of how much to charge is faced by all businessmen, from barbers to bankers. If you charge too much, you will price yourself out of the market. If you charge too little, your expenses will be larger than your income. In either case, the result is the same—your column will fail.

Obviously, threading the price needle correctly is no easy task. And many a superb column has gone down the tubes because of poor marketing and pricing. Unfortunately, no one has yet come up with a foolproof formula for pricing a column.

There are two basic ways of determining a fair price for your column:

1. Make a "guesstimate" of the number of newspapers you think you can sell your column to. Then calculate your own cost (minus your time) for producing X number of columns and sending them out, plus the cost of bookkeeping, collections on overdue accounts, phone calls, and other overhead. Then divide the number of client papers into that figure to determine your "nut," or "break-even" figure.

Now tack on what you feel is a fair fee (we suggest 20% for a starter). In other words, if you come up with a per-column, per-paper cost of $1.00 per column, add 20 cents for each to determine your price to the publisher.

2. Get a post office box and send inquiries to as many syndicates and individual columnists as possible who advertise in *E&P* and other trade journals. State that you are interested in seeing one of their columns and their rates. Don't state that you are another columnist. Let them assume you are a newspaper editor or publisher. You haven't lied, but you'll get plenty of input this way.

When the columnists' sales packets come in, check them out to see how much each is asking for a column based on number of words and accompanying photos, illustrations, etc.

Make up a chart and then calculate the average price, adjusting it to the estimated length of your own columns. Use your own judgment to add other factors, such as the quality of the columns compared to yours, then come up with your own price. Compare it to your estimated cost of production and you will be able to determine the likelihood of making a profit.

Keep in mind that all of the above is highly speculative, just as loans made by banks to new businesses are highly speculative. They depend on a lot of intangibles—estimated sales, estimated growth, the health of the economy in general, etc. In this sense, syndicating your own column is like starting any other business. It is part inspiration, part hard work, and part luck. You'll need all three ingredients, plus a certain amount of capital, to have a 50-50 shot at success.

You'll find that columns sold directly to papers by individual columnists range in price per column from 50 cents to $20 or more. Those that are at the high end of the totem pole are usually political and consumer interest columns, produced by lobbyists and others in state capitals and in a position to report on the inner workings of state government.

Use sales incentives

Newspaper editors may fancy themselves knights in shining

armor, out to right the wrongs of society, but in practice, most editors spend 99 percent of their work days dealing with much more mundane problems—like how to get and keep more readers, and how to stay within a strict editorial budget.

Today's editor is part journalist, part businessman. When he hires a new reporter, or buys a free-lance article, or contracts for a regular column such as yours, he's interested in how much it will cost. Your job, then, is to show him *how much he can save.*

The trial offer

The trial offer is used by virtually every major magazine publisher, by book-of-the-month clubs, by record clubs, even by furniture stores. Stated in its simplest form, it goes like this: "Sign up for this new column on a 10-week trial basis and get 20 percent off our regular price." There are many variations, but the idea is to give the editor a discount for trying your product. At the end of the 10-week period, you simply continue to send the column and bill monthly at the regular rate.

Chances are the editor and the business department will continue to use the column without comment, especially if it has "found its niche" in the daily layout of the paper, and especially if it is proving popular with readers.

Don't automatically assume that if the editor advises you he is dropping the column, you've lost the ball game. Often readers write in or telephone when they can't find a particular column. When that happens you may get a frantic call and a "rush" order.

The money-back offer

If you are a bit of a gambler, you can increase the initial acceptance of your column by including in your presentations an offer to give papers their money back at the end of the trial period if they elect not to continue. You will have to give a certain percentage of the money back. There are always some editors and publishers, especially in small towns, who take advantage of such an offer with no intention of continuing the column after the trial period. But the other side of the coin is that the money-back offer will probably double the number of papers which agree to take your column, and the bottom line will be greater overall revenue during this period plus many more long-term customers, despite the drop-outs.

Getting papers to carry your column doesn't mean you've got it made. The final gauge of your success will be your balance sheet at the end of a year.

Here are some pointers to keep your column in the black once it is off and running:

• Keep regular books and records. Hire a CPA and request a regular monthly balance sheet and figures on accounts payable and accounts receivable.

• Hire an accounts receivable agency (different from a collection agency) to deal with your client newspapers. Or hire a good bookkeeper who will work with your account and function as your collections manager. Adopt a firm collections policy and be sure to spell it out in writing to all client newspapers when you sign them on. Then there will be no disagreement later.

• Don't be afraid to cut off a paper that falls several months behind in paying. Remember that a customer who doesn't pay is worse than no customer at all because he costs you a good deal more money.

• Always make sure your client newspapers have at least four or five columns on file in advance and advise them that if they do not receive a fresh column each day or week to call your office. Then send one out express mail, special delivery, or UPS, depending on the location of the paper. Even if the cost eats up an entire month's revenue from that client, chalk it up as the cost of doing business. You'll keep your clients happy and when the editors get together at professional meetings, they'll always have good things instead of bad things to say about your operation.

• Give papers the option of getting your column set in type or in typewritten version. Do not sent Xerox copies. Spend a few dollars and have each column printed (both typewritten and typeset versions) at a local speedy printer. The cost is just a few dollars and it will keep your columns looking as if they were produced by a professional organization. It will also save you a lot of time, and as the old cliche goes, "Time is money."

• As soon as your mailing list grows past 20, check with local mailing houses to find out about the cost of having your list automated (either on metal transfer plates, IBM file cards, or on computer). Usually the cost of having a mailing house keep your mailing list current, in Zip Code order, and stuffing and mailing each column will run from 1 to 3 cents per piece, thanks to their automated machinery. Again, you save yourself time and the drudgery of hand processing each client's column each day or week.

• Earlier we suggested that your samples include typewritten columns, plus columns set in type in widths of 11, 14, and 20 picas. This may sound costly, but if you go to a typographer who has modern computerized typesetting equipment, he can call your column from a floppy disc memory system with the touch of a button and have "it" reset in various widths for a few dollars extra. Not only that, you can save each column on the memory disc and if you ever need additional copies for reprints, you can have the column reset for a fraction of the original setting cost.

• Should you buy your own typesetting equipment? Definitely not until you are sure your column has established itself and the number of client newspapers is growing. Even then, you don't want to spend $15,000 or $20,000 for the latest state-of-the-art phototypesetting equipment if it will sit idle 90 percent of the time.

• Continually update your sales packet, especially when you start getting unsolicited letters of praise from editors and readers. Reprint these (with permission, of course) and add them to your sales packet. If you have enough, take selected quotes from the better letters and make up a separate sheet with them.

• As you pick up client newspapers, recontact papers that elected not to carry your column earlier. Nothing succeeds like success, and editors hate to think they've missed out on a good thing. When they see that your column is hot, many will want to climb aboard the bandwagon.

• Don't wait until your column's popularity begins to wane before you start planning for its successor. Everything has a lifespan, be it human or the creation of humans, and columns are no exception. They usually follow a bell-shaped curve, growing in popularity, then leveling off, and eventually falling off.

Selling your second column idea will be twice as easy as the first one, because now you not only have a track record, you have a nucleus of customers, most of whom will pick up your new offering. Not only that, you will have learned all kinds of tricks of the trade over and above the advice in this book, and the second time around, you can get your column off and flying much faster and with less wasted motion and expense.

Conclusion:

What to expect

You may entertain grandiose ideas of becoming another Walter Lippman, Rona Barrett, or Irv Kupcinet—demigods all, at least in their own special worlds. After all, power of one form or another is what many seek. Money is necessary, but nonetheless secondary. It is simply a means to achieving an end. But whether you seek a form of power or just money, it is certainly the measuring stick by which our society gauges our success in almost every endeavor. That's why our heroes, such as the stars of the sports world, are able to command multi-year contracts which make them overnight millionaires.

In the case of writers, two varieties of the breed sit atop the heap. The first is the author of the best-selling book, be it a novel or a nonfiction work. (Imagine earning royalties of 10% on a book like *Jaws,* which at last report had topped 2 million in print!) The second echelon superstar among writers is none other than the *syndicated columnist.*

There are plenty of other writers who do pretty well. Star

reporters on major metropolitan daily papers usually earn double the income of their counterparts in the newsroom, but that still only puts them in the $40,000 to $50,000 range; top ad copywriters can reach the six-figure bracket on occasion, as can speech writers and public relations men. But in the main, writers are a poorly paid lot indeed.

Given these facts, you should be pleased that you have decided to take a crack at producing (and possibly distributing) your own syndicated column. But before you start counting your money, hold on. Within the ranks of the 1,200 or so persons who can legitimately call themselves syndicated columnists are tax returns which span the spectrum, so to speak.

Not every syndicated columnist is as well known or as handsomely paid as Ann Landers or Dr. Joyce Brothers. A handful of the most sought-after make big bucks. The majority, on the other hand, earn a good, but certainly not great, income. And some consider their column simply as a second income— that's right, they have another, full-time job!

As for the top columnists, most are quick to admit that their world is not nearly as glamorous as you might imagine. Film critic Rex Reed summed up the feelings of many of his colleagues in Ross Firestone's book, *The Success Trip:*

> Writing is a hard profession. There are no intrinsic pleasures about the writing itself. The pleasures come from the success of the writing. . . . I hate the discipline of writing and I hate the discipline of deadlines. [Sometimes] I'm searching on Sunday night for things to turn in on Monday morning . . . this is the nightmare of newspaper work. But in return, I have absolute autonomy. Nobody tells me what to do. I have no boss. I make a hell of a lot of money. And I'm famous.

Well, we've pretty much said all there is to say. The rest you'll have to learn on your own. So, if you are still ready and willing to give your hopes and plans for your own syndicated column a whirl, have a go at it, and good luck!

Index

A

accountants, 58–59, 87
advertising, 30, 82–83
agriculture, 11, 14
American Features Syndicate, 18
animals, 11, 14, 15, 18
armed forces, 11
arts, 11, 14, 15, 16, 19, 21
Authenticated News
    International, 18
auto expenses, 55

B

benefits, fringe, 51–53
bookkeeping, 53–59, 87
business, 12, 14, 15, 16, 17, 19,
    21

C

CPM, 70
celebrities, 13
Chicago Sun-Times, 44
Chicago Tribune/New York
    News Syndicate, 18, 67
child care, 12, 13
cliches, 34
columnists, 4
columns
    daily, 49
    definition of, 3
    developing, 7–21, 23–30
    developing, 7–21, 23–30
    general interest, 7–8, 20
    sample, 10, 68, 74, 80, 88
    seasonal, 48–49
    selling, 5, 73–77, 79–89

special interest, 8
weekly, 49
writing, 31–39
commissions, 70
competition, 70
contacts, 24, 42
contracts, 70–71
copyright laws, 63–64
correspondence, 68, 74
Cosell, Howard, 7
cost, selling, 9
crafts, 13, 14
credentials, 10

D

deadlines, 49, 68
dictionaries, 33
direct-mail, 82–83, 88
Douglas Whiting, Ltd., 21

E

Editor & Publisher, 82–83
*Editor and Publisher Syndicate
    Directory,* 10
editorials, 3
editors, 68–69, 76, 85–86
education, 13, 14
entertainment expenses, 56
errors, 43
evaluating columns, 23–28
expenses
    entertainment, 56
    miscellaneous, 56–57
    travel, 55–56

F

features, 3, 71

fees, 5, 9, 70
freedom of information, 63
freedom of the press, 63
fringe benefits, 51–53

G

General Features, 18
gifts, 51–53
goals, 32
Goodwin, Dave, & Associates,
    18
Greenwich Features, Inc., 18

H

head, standing, 3
health, 15, 16, 18, 19
Hemingway, Ernest, 28
hobbies, 10, 12, 13, 14, 15, 16,
    20
holidays, 13
hotel bills, 55
humor, 35–36

I

ideas, selling, 73–77
ideas, topic, 11–17
illustrations, 50, 71, 80
income, 5, 9
Internal Revenue Service, 53–59
interviews, 36–39
    telephone, 39
invasion of privacy, 62–63

J

journalism, new, 23–30
journalism schools, 26

K

King Features Syndicate, 19, 67,
    79
knowledge, columnist's, 23

L

legal issues, 61–64, 76
length, 29–30
letterhead, 75
libel, 38–39, 61–62
library research, 9
lifestyles, 12, 15, 18
literature, 12, 16
logs, 49, 84
Los Angeles Times Syndicate, 19

M

magazines, 28
marketing, 5, 9, 30, 73–77, 79–89
McNaught Syndicate, Inc., 19
media kits, 80
Mel Martin Enterprises, 19
Mid-Continent Feature
    Syndicate, 19
money-back offers, 86–87

N

NC News Service, 20
National Catholic News Service,
    19
National Feature Syndicate, 19
National Newspaper Syndicate,
    19
New York Graphic, 4
New York Herald Tribune, 29
New York Times, 4
news, 8

news services, 67, 69
news story formula, 26–27
Newsco Press Features, Inc., 20
Newspaper Enterprise Assn., 20
newspapers, 9 (see also
    individual newspapers)
North American Newspaper
    Alliance, 20
notebooks, 37
Numismatic Information
    Service, 20

O

Oceanic Press Service, 20
outlines, 32–33

P

packaging, 73–74, 79–82
paragraphing, 35
paraphrasing, 33
personalities, 13, 15, 21
photography, 50, 56–57, 71, 80
planning, 47–48, 50, 89
press cards, 51
pricing, 69–71, 84–85
privacy, invasion of, 62–63
protection, territorial, 70
public figures, 62
public interest, 23
Publishers-Hall Syndicate, 20
puns, 34–35

Q

queries, 10, 74
quotations, 33

R

radio, 8
rates, 69–71
Readers' Guide to Periodical Literature, 9
records, 53–59, 87
recreation, 12, 14, 15, 17, 19
Register & Tribune Syndicate, 20
religion, 12, 13, 14, 17, 19, 20
repetition, 36
reporters, 41–45
research, 9, 57
resumes, 75, 80
reviews, 3
Roget's Thesaurus, 33

S

salaries, 70
sales, 5, 73–77, 79–89
scheduling, 48–50
sciences, 11, 13, 18, 20
slang, 34
sources (see contacts)
spelling, 42
sports, 12, 15, 16, 18, 20
staffs, newspaper, 8–9
standing head, 3
statistics, 35
style, 48
subject matter, 7–17, 42
syndicated features, 71
syndicates, 4, 18–21, 67–71

T

tape recorders, 37

taxes, 53–59, 84
technology, 14, 17
television, 8
topic ideas, 11–17
Trans-World News Service, 21
travel, 17, 18, 21
travel expenses, 55–56
trial offers, 86
typography, 80, 88

U

under cover, 44–45
United Feature Syndicate, Inc., 21
U.S. News Service, 21

V

Vandeville News, 4
Village Voice, 29, 44–45
visual aids, 50, 56–57, 71, 80

W

Washington Post, 4
weather, 17
Winchell, Walter, 4–5
Wolfe, Tom, 28
Women's News Service, 21
writing ability, 26, 31
writing columns, 31–39

XYZ

Zodiac News Service, 21